A PROMISE TO GOD

The story of Pastor Cam Iverson
12/12/13–11/30/88

BY LAURA M. PORRAS

Laura M Porras

" . . . *well done, good and faithful servant* . . ."
Matthew 25:23

TATE PUBLISHING, LLC

Thank you so
much for being here
tonight. Don't ever loose
Faith!
GOD Bless!
Laura

This book is dedicated to the memory of
Pastor Campbell Iverson
And to his lovely wife Gladys

FOREWORD

"If you will spare my life, I will serve you for the rest of my days on earth." That is what Campbell Iverson prayed as he was on his way to the hospital in June of 1965 at the age of 51. Cam had suffered a massive heart attack that evening and spent the next month on the verge of death. *God does not forget our promises to Him.*

There were many times while doing my research that I felt guided in very specific directions. I am a woman of faith, but I do not flaunt it or throw it in people's faces. While writing this book, I learned more about faith, deep faith, than any church ever taught me. I walked away from organized religion years ago for personal reasons. I have always lived my life doing the best I can, being nice to those around me and helping out where I can. I share little bits of my faith along the road. I believe that everything happens for a reason. We may not understand it or like it very much, but there is a reason for it, and we must accept that.

When Cam's grandson, Jon Bellows Jr., came to me about writing this book, I was afraid. It wasn't a lack of confidence or a lack of faith; it was the challenge it involved. Being a poet, I was reaching so far out of my comfort zone and writing about someone and something that I knew absolutely nothing about. I have been Jon's friend and a friend of other members of his extended family for a few years now, but that is as far as it went.

I spoke with my family and friends and got everyone's opinion on the subject. Some people said don't bother, it will take time away from your poetry, and others said go for it. My dad was the most excited. Then I did what I should have done in the first place. I prayed about it. The bottom line is that you never know until you try.

Bob Iverson, Cam's younger brother, said it best to me

when he stated, "Quitters never win, and winners never quit." In that same conversation, he also said to me, "An angel has come down and touched you on the shoulder." I absolutely got chills. This warm and tingly feeling went through my entire body, and I knew I was doing the right thing.

I didn't want to turn down this project out of fear. Fear holds so many of us back from reaching our true potential.

I hope that you enjoy the story you are about to read. Every word of it is true, and that is what makes it so amazing. There are many people still alive today who know this family personally and can quote much of this story inside and out. There are others who have never heard it before. Like Cam said in many of his sermons, "I don't know why God wants me to tell this story, but if it reaches out to you, then that is all the reason I need."

BEFORE CAMPBELL

Mother of Courage

This story begins with a tiny Norwegian woman by the name of Anna Marie Kristiansen, 9/22/1879–10/6/1947, the eldest daughter of Kristian Kornelius Mikkelsen and Anne Kristine Nilsdatter. In her youth, Anna tended to the cows, fetched water, washed, cleaned, and cooked. She was a very hard worker and being the oldest had a lot of responsibility.

Anna always looked forward to Sundays, because that was when the daily routine would change. When services were held at the parish church of Vassas, the family would row five miles each way by boat across the waters of Bindalsfjorden to attend. Her family showed so much devotion to their faith in that simple act alone. These days, we find it hard to just roll out of bed on Sunday morning and drive a couple of miles.

Let me be the first to tell you, that woman had faith. In the face of adversity and persecution, most of us would run and hide—not Anna. She faced it head on with a Bible in her hands and a deep love and devotion for Someone she had never met in her heart. I watched a video about Anna and her quest for her family's salvation. It was called Mother of Courage. She vowed not to stop until everyone in her family had taken the Lord into their lives. Believe me, she had quite the hard road ahead of her.

Anna had been engaged to a fisherman by the name of Nels. They intended to marry and raise a family. Nels left to find work and a home when an accidental drowning in the fjords of Norway took his life early. Anna was absolutely heartbroken. Looking at the possibility of staying single forever, she steadfastly did her chores and farm work, hoping that God would use her life.

While out herding the cows one afternoon in the pastures of Vikestad, she had a vision of an index finger pointing to an open Bible with children from a foreign culture and race in the background. These children weren't European and looked rather Oriental. She didn't know what it meant, but she vowed to fulfill that vision somehow.

Karl Johan Hagerup Iversen, 10/22/1868, (his name was later Americanized to Carl Iverson) was introduced to Anna second hand by her younger sister's fiancé Oluf Jakobsen. Oluf had mentioned to Carl that Anna was still single. Carl's father had been from Vikestad, and it was well known that Kristian Kornelius Mikkelsen had lovely daughters.

Carl began communicating with Anna by mail, and when he returned to his homeland in December of 1909, he asked for her hand in marriage. He wanted her to marry him and go far away from their native Norway to live in Canada and raise a family.

Anna was uncertain about leaving her home. She was afraid because she didn't know any language besides her native Norwegian and had only gone to school for two years. Anna did what any Christian woman would do and prayed about it. Remembering her vision she thought, "Perhaps if I marry Carl, I will find these children in the new country to which he will take me." Anna agreed to marry him.

On February 6, 1910, Anna and Carl were joined in matrimony in the parish church of Vassas. Within just 10 days of marrying, they boarded a Canadian ship and immigrated to North America.

In early 1911, Anna gave birth to a daughter who tragically died in infancy. This was a source of deep grief and disappointment for both of them.

1912–1940

Carl and Anna settled in Saskatchewan, Canada by 1912. The children there didn't look Oriental. Anna's vision from the fields was always in the back of her mind; she knew it would have to wait. They both worked the land as best they could, and Anna bore four children for him. Adeline Engara, 5/22/12; Campbell Astrup, 12/12/13; Hegge Marius, 12/21/14; and Ruth Adelia, 5/5/18. Another child was stillborn in 1916.

The Canadian winters were long and harsh, and Anna's health was very fragile. She had an open abscess in her side that absolutely would not heal. Life was rewarding, but they had to work very hard. Carl was making his livelihood by crafting leather goods. He suffered a devastating fire in his workshop and lost many materials, tools, and personal family documents from Norway. All of this combined with Anna's need for better medical attention took its toll, and a decision was made to start over again in America.

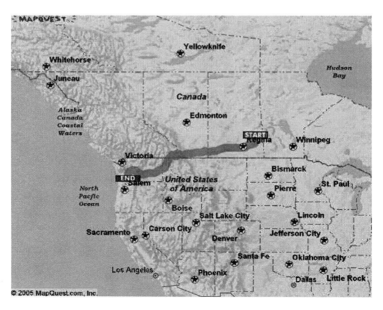

On November 17, 1920, the family boarded the Great Northern Railway and made the 1242-mile, two-day trip to Washington State. Carl had two nephews in the Seattle area, so family was relatively close to their final destination in Yelm, about an hour and a half southeast.

Anna noticed right away that the children from her vision in Norway didn't look Oriental here either. Her vision would once again have to wait to be fulfilled. Carl and Anna prepared the land for berry farming and began their life full of misery and miracles alike.

In 1922, with the help of family and friends, Carl built the family home at what was known at that time as Iverson's Corner. Some of his land is still owned and occupied by his descendants on Yelm Avenue. Their fifth child, Robert Oliver, 1/15/25, was born here.

The Original Sinner

"And the LORD God commanded the man saying, 'Of every tree of the garden you may freely eat,' 'but of the tree of the knowledge of good and evil you shall not eat, for in the day that you eat of it you shall surely die.'" Genesis 2:16–17

Adam and Eve succumbed to the devil, thus leading to the temptation and fall of man which is spelled out in Genesis 3:1–24.

It all has to start somewhere.

Campbell Astrup Iverson was born on December 12, 1913 in Buchanan, Saskatchewan, Canada. He was the second of five children.

Original sin is a very complicated issue. According to the Bible, we are all born sinners. That is why Jesus died for us, so that we may be saved and all go to heaven. Cam took that honor far beyond what Jesus intended.

Cam's official Birth Certificate

Cam's Registration of Birth

Carl, Adeline, Anna, & Cam

Cam attended the Yelm Public Schools from 1st grade in 1920 through the end of 8th grade in 1928. Due to a school building fire in 1941, all of his academic records were lost. From the information I was able to obtain, he was an average student, not great, but not terrible either.

Back in those days, getting as far as the 8th grade was a good thing. Education was not as much of a priority as keeping the farm going or looking for work was. In today's society, we stress education for the betterment of everyone, and you can't get a decent job without a good one.

Letter from Cam's School

It is, however, amazing what a man with an 8th grade education can accomplish.

Half Pint

We are all victims of circumstance in some way or another. Cam grew up in a household riddled with both violence and faith. What a contradiction! He would watch his father go into the barn and come back out wiping his face.

The power of influence was very strong, and curiosity eventually overcame him. Cam followed in his father's footsteps and started making his own treks out to the barn. There he found his Dad's stash of alcohol. First, Cam just took little sips, but it wasn't too long before those sips became a full-blown addiction to the beast.

In his teens, Cam also learned how to make his own alcohol. He even had a homemade still upstairs in his bedroom! How is that for being desperate?

It is no mystery to the residents of Yelm exactly what kind of person Cam Iverson was. He flat out admitted that if there was trouble brewing in this town, he was probably at the very heart of it.

This is the same man who reeked of alcohol 24 hours a day, 7 days a week. Cam started drinking in the 7th grade and ended up dropping out of school the following year. His nickname from the town folk was "Half Pint," not for any lack of stature, but instead due to his incredible ability to consume alcohol. He was heavily addicted to alcohol and felt as though he had to have it! Every bad habit he could have, he did. No matter how hard he tried to kick his addictions, he just couldn't do it.

This is the same man who knew more foul language than most of us speak in a month. This is also the same man who almost did time up in Monroe for stealing chickens from henhouses—yes, you heard me right, chickens. His daughter Sharon also told me stories of the rabbits he would steal for breeding!

At that particular point in his life, Cam would do just about anything to get a drink. I tried to obtain more information about his thievery, but no one in this town had records going back that far.

Rumor had it that Cam spent time at the Washington Reformatory in Monroe. After careful research and many questions, I found that it was just that, a rumor. Due to a lack of records, both in Yelm and at the Reformatory, I never could find out why.

Somehow, by the grace of God, he escaped that route and went on to do great things with his life.

The Washington State Reformatory Unit was opened in 1910 and is still in use today, although it has expanded tremendously. The entire Monroe Correctional Complex has four units consisting of the Washington State Reformatory; the Twin Rivers Corrections Unit, which was opened in 1984; the Minimum Security Unit, opened in 1997; and the Special Offenders Unit that opened in 1981. Combined, they house a total of approximately 2,044 male inmates and employ over 1,000 staff members.

The Complex is responsible for the custody, security, classification, education, inmate work programs, health care, (both in patient and out patient), mental health programs, food service, maintenance, personnel, social responsibility programs, recreation, library and law library, volunteer services, and visiting/ extended family visiting of its inmates. OCO accounting is also housed there now. The facility has been called the "University of Another Chance" and is the largest employer in the city of Monroe.

Carl became a US Citizen on October 4, 1929; Anna remained a citizen of Norway until her death.

Home had been described as absolutely "hell on earth!" Fifteen years of darkness followed the Iverson family. Tragedy after tragedy befell them. Papa was so consumed with his anger, frustration, and booze, that he seemed to be a raving mad lunatic. Their home was bleeding, broken, and sick from the inside out.

All that was about to change.

Who would have ever thought that one woman named Anna Iverson could make a difference in so many lives?

At Cam's lowest point, Anna took her faith to the highest level. She would weep and pray over his clothes and underwear anointing them with simple oil from the garage, claiming healing for him from his alcoholism. *"God, save my boy at any cost!"*

Anna would say. Cam would yell and spit out hateful words to her, telling her to *"Go to Hell!"* but he also listened. It was a very slow and gradual process. With every tear and prayer from Anna, Cam was coming closer to his beautiful destiny.

With miracle after miracle occurring in his family, Cam was bound to hear that inaudible voice calling him to service in the Lord's name. I will tell you more about the miracles a little bit later.

Sunday School scriptures were starting to get under his skin as they really bothered him. He didn't like hearing them. Cam knew right from wrong and he also knew that these words he was hearing were much stronger than he was. He could feel the power building in his veins.

One Sunday evening after service, the Pastor of his church went to him and said, "Young man, you are under conviction! Come to the altar." Cam didn't feel as though he was. It took some persuading, but he followed the Pastor, despite his desire to run and hide. He had been in the back of the church at the time and probably smelled like alcohol.

Once at the altar, Cam fell to his knees and cried. I imagine the chill running down his spine as the warmth of the love of God entered his very soul. Everyone in the congregation was praising God and putting their hands on Cam. Salvation was in the air.

All Cam could think of was how much he wanted to be delivered. He didn't like living the life he was following. He was ashamed and afraid. Four days later as he was in the barn milking the cows, he realized that he hadn't had his morning cigarette. The joy of the Lord suddenly flooded his soul, and it followed him from that day forward. Cam could often be heard saying, "Serving Christ is realistic and tangible." That is exactly how he chose to lead the rest of his life.

A few weeks later on a Sunday morning, Cam, the new convert, was asked to give his testimony during that evening's service. Cam was so nervous because of his speech impediment; he had a terrible problem with stuttering. He didn't want to embarrass himself by stuttering through his testimony. That Sunday afternoon he wrote out a speech and eliminated all the words and letters that he knew would trip him up.

As he spoke, Satan plagued his tongue, and he stuttered on nearly every word. Cam wanted to run out of that church and never come back. After he finished his short testimony, Mother Dickerson, one of the fine ladies of the church, came up to him and said, "I really enjoyed your testimony."

You can imagine what was going through Cam's mind at that time. Although he was embarrassed about his stuttering through the testimony, he was also filled with a great sense of pride. After receiving the compliment from Mother Dickerson, Cam prayed, "Lord, stutter or no stutter, every opportunity I have I am going to speak for you." From that day forward, that is exactly what he did.

After that commitment was made, his stuttering virtually disappeared.

Anna's Abscess

Michael Levine's, "Miracles", states the following:

Aquinas (*Summa Contra Gentiles,* III) says "those things are properly called miracles which are done by divine agency beyond the order commonly observed in nature *(praeter ordinem communiter observatum in rebus)*." A miracle, philosophically speaking, is never a mere coincidence no matter how extraordinary or significant. (If you miss a plane and the plane crashes, that is not a miracle unless God intervened in the natural course of events causing you to miss the flight.) A miracle is a supernaturally (divinely) caused event - an event (ordinarily) different from what would have occurred in the normal ("natural") course of events. It is a divine overriding of, or interference with, the natural order. As such, it need not be extraordinary, marvelous or significant, and it must be something other than a coincidence, no matter how remarkable - unless the "coincidence" itself is caused by divine intervention (i.e., not really a coincidence at all). Miracles, however, are ordinarily understood to be not just products of divine intervention in the natural order, but extraordinary, marvelous and significant as well. Thus, Aquinas says a miracle is "beyond the order commonly observed;" and Dr. Eric Mascall says that the word "miracle" "signifies in Christian theology a striking interposition of divine power by which the operations of the ordinary course of nature are overruled, suspended, or modified" (Chamber's Encyclopedia).

During my research I read a few books about miracles. My favorite was "Miracles and Other Wonders" by Charles Sellier. Many of the stories below follow right along with the complete mystery of why these things happen. All I can say is that there is a higher power at work here.

Anna had an open abscess in her left side that would not heal. The doctors in Tacoma had told Carl that nothing could be done. The abscess kept draining month after month, but Anna believed that God would heal her. She asked Carl for two cents to buy a stamp to send a request for prayer to an Evangelist who was praying for the sick.

Carl was furious and refused to give her permission to write the letter or buy the stamp. Anna stood up to him and reminded him of how he had spent money on doctors to get her well and yet she was no better. She asked him to give her the two cents now and at least try this to make her well. He finally relented, and she sent off her letter for prayer.

The evangelist responded to Anna's request by sending her a handkerchief in the mail. This special hanky was anointed with oil and had been prayed upon and blessed by the man. She was instructed to place the anointed handkerchief on her wound each day.

One night, a miracle of faith took place. Anna said that a burning sensation began in the open sore and continued all night long. By morning, she was able to stand upright, something she hadn't been able to do for many years. The abscess began to go away, and in a few weeks her side was completely healed.

Carl and Anna's relationship was often tumultuous, difficult, and sometimes violent. However, Anna never spoke a negative word about him, even after finding out that he was cheating on her and knowing that he was beating the boys, especially Cam. She had her undying faith and a little black Bible to guide her.

Every night she would read from her Bible in Norwegian. All of her children grew up listening to this from infancy on. She had been brought up in the Lutheran Church of Norway and sought faith outlets here in our then tiny town. Most of her time had been spent on their farm, because she didn't speak a word of English. She wanted to socialize, but there was always so much she had to do.

A family friend invited Anna to a tent meeting across from the Assembly of God Church downtown. Not having a vehicle, she walked the mile and a half to the meeting. At this tent meeting, Anna finally learned that she had to be "Born Again." It was such a joyous revelation for her. Carl was absolutely furious with her. He grew to hate God and all those who served Him. He cursed Anna, and he cursed the church. Carl threatened her not to attend and said her place was in their home cooking and caring for their family. These threats only made her faith that much stronger.

Bob's Eye

Bob was out chopping wood one day when a piece with a nail in it flew up to his face. The nail hit him squarely in the eye, piercing his eyelid. Blood was flowing out as he ran to his mother's side. Anna placed her hands on his eye and cried out to God for help. Miraculously, the bleeding stopped. She washed out his eye and to this day, he has never had a single problem with it.

Bob recalled to me a story of when he was a young boy helping his Dad in the berry field. Carl had lost his prized pocket watch somewhere in the vast expanse of berries and bush. He was frantic to find it and had asked the boys to help him. Bob prayed, "Dear God, please help me to find the watch." Low and behold, after some searching and faith, the watch was found.

Bob also suffered from a very serious condition called rheumatic fever, which is an acute inflammatory disease. It usually follows a streptococcal infection of the throat. This type of condition can be deadly if left untreated. Of course, Bob had Anna and God on his side. The treatment and her daily prayers assisted in his recovery.

In the late 1990's, Bob was diagnosed with Prostate Cancer. After his diagnosis, he went away for a weekend to pray, fast, and ask God what to do. While in prayer, the message he received was to "go home and have communion every day." After one solid year of prayer and communion each morning with his wife, he was completely cancer free.

Bob is the youngest of the Iverson children and a full 12 years younger than Cam. He was called very early in life to a Musical Ministry, playing the piano, accordion, and singing. He is still very active in the Christian Musical Ministries, with his wife Maggie, and as he sings and plays, he remembers his Mama!

Years ago he and Maggie had their own TV and Radio ministry that was very effective. Recently, at 80 years old, Bob and his wife recorded their first musical gospel CD together.

Hegge's Bolt of Light

When Hegge was 12 years old, he, Ruth, and Cam were out playing at a neighbor's house when a storm suddenly raged. A huge bolt of lightning hit a nearby tree setting it on fire. Scared, they all ran for home. Ruth took the path and ran as hard as she could. Cam and Hegge took a short cut through the fence.

Just as Hegge grabbed hold of the barbed wire, another lightning bolt struck it, and he was knocked to the ground unconscious. Cam took off across the fields to tell his parents. Carl, very upset and sure that he would die, carried Hegge home.

Hegge was in a coma for days. With each day that passed, Anna would walk confidently into his room, lay her hands on her unconscious son's body and declare, "Jesus Christ makes you whole!"

One day, Hegge opened his eyes and was soon up and around again. His Mother's faith in God had healed him and another miracle was recorded within the family.

Hegge's Bees

The Iverson's Bees were the best controlled in the whole Bee Club, according to Mr. Henderson at the school where they attended. Hegge had always said that the bees were his friends and that they would never sting him. He and Cam had been out at the hives playing with them one afternoon.

The bees were crawling all over their arms when suddenly hundreds of them swarmed out and attacked Hegge. He was only able to walk maybe five or six feet before he fell to the ground. After hearing his screams and rushing out to see what had happened, Anna, with Cam's help, carried him to the kitchen.

Ruth screamed that he was turning blue, and Anna told Bob to run and tell Carl to send for the doctor. Knowing that time was very short, Anna did what she knew best and prayed.

"Dear God, what shall I do? He'll die before the doctor gets here! Lord, you are my Counselor!" She paused for a moment and then said, "Thank you, Lord! Thank you, Lord! The cream!"

Anna, going on her faith alone, grabbed a pitcher of cream from the pantry and began to pour it all over Hegge. Half of it went down his mouth, and the rest all over his body. She asked the children to help her prop him up.

As the doctor finally arrived, he exclaimed, "Lady, what in the world is this?"

"It's cream," she answered calmly.

"Who told you to use cream?"

She replied, "Well, I knew that he would die before you got here, so I asked God what to do, and He told me to use cream."

"Have you ever read a medical journal?" the doctor countered.

"I don't know what you are talking about; what is that?" Anna asked.

"A book on medicine, has anyone ever told you that cream is an antidote for bee venom?" The Doctor had a look of pure disbelief on his face at that time.

"No, I didn't know that; I just did what God said." Anna stood defiantly.

Stunned, he asked her, "Do you mean to tell me that God gave you those instructions? Incredible! Well at any rate you have saved the boy's life. He would have been dead if you hadn't given him the cream." The Doctor didn't know what to think at that point but gave Anna her due credit for doing the right thing at the right time.

Once again, Anna's faith had lead to saving another of her son's lives.

Ruth's Ankle

At the age of 11, Cam's sister Ruth was playing baseball when she sprained her ankle. A year later, Tuberculosis of the bone **(Skeletal Tuberculosis:** Tuberculous osteomyelitis) in the ankle set in. TB of the ankle is uncommon, but the sprain exacerbated the problem. The infection was more than likely present in a dormant pulmonary form, and came to light after the injury. The family was to find out later that Ruth wasn't the only one carrying this disease.

In June of 1931, when Ruth was 12, a bone specialist in

Tacoma was called upon to operate on her. Three ankle joints were subsequently removed, and she was forced to be on crutches and in casts for the next seven years.

During this long period of time she helped her mother in the kitchen to the best of her abilities, all the while listening to Anna's stories of their native land and in particular the story of her vision about the children. This was a very intriguing story to Ruth.

Anything she could do while sitting was done to help out. Ruth didn't like the feeling of being "useless." There was so much that had to be done.

Anna would often pray for Ruth's healing and would say: "Ruth, give God your life, maybe He would have you to become a missionary." Ruth's reply was always: "Mama, don't be silly—God needs for me to have two good feet if I am to work for Him!"

Anna kept praying for Ruth and her future. Somewhere down deep in her soul, she knew great things were yet to happen for her daughter.

Eventually after a second operation, the doctors thought that they would have to amputate Ruth's foot. Her condition had gotten much worse than anyone had ever expected.

Ruth was alone in her bedroom very late one night. God was dealing with her to be fully committed to His service. He spoke to her and told her to take her cast off because He was going to heal her. It was then that she made her uncompromising commitment to Jesus Christ. If He so chose, she would be a missionary to the part of the world to which the little children of Anna's vision had belonged—Asia.

That night, Ruth walked without the aid of crutches for the first time in years. Due to the prayers of Anna, Ruth was miraculously healed. The miracles didn't stop there.

The following morning Ruth was able to walk down the stairs without her usual "clomping" noise. That was the first thing the rest of the family noticed. Once she made her appearance in the kitchen, Carl was so astounded that he left the table, absolutely speechless!

Anna knew of her daughter's healing. She had felt the presence of God the night before. She knew He was at Ruth's side that night.

Hegge's Tuberculosis

While Ruth was having operations on her ankle, Hegge, in his early 20's at the time, fell ill with Tuberculosis of the lungs that spread to his spine. He wasted away to a mere 97 pounds, nearly dying.

Tuberculosis (TB) is officially defined as a chronic or acute bacterial infection that primarily attacks the lungs, but which may also affect the kidneys, bones, lymph nodes, and brain, with the spine being the most common skeletal presentation accounting for 50–60% of those cases.

In the US from 10–15 million people are actually infected with the germs that cause TB, but only 10 percent of those will get sick with it. After someone is infected, the risk remains for the duration of his or her life. There is evidence that TB has been around since the beginning of time and it was more than likely a common disease in ancient Egypt.

"In popular representation in the late nineteenth century, consumptions were perceived as bourgeois illnesses that spiritualized the sufferer. The illness might create an ethereal invalid of the woman as shown in an illustration accompanying a poem on consumption by William Cullen Bryant, or spark creative genius in a man, as with [a] character from a short story in McClure's Magazine. Such images of consumptives were meant to convey the presence of a powerful and consuming force within their earthly bodies." (Ott)

Hegge had been sick for 8 years with TB. Often times he could be found out on the veranda just bathing in the sun. He had been in three different sanitariums with 36 different doctors attending to his care. There was absolutely no hope of recovery.

Anna visited him as often as she could. She always put her hands on his chest and declared in faith, "Hegge, Jesus Christ makes you whole!"

One morning at 2 A.M., he was awakened suddenly. As he lay there still, he was aware of the presence of the Lord. His heart was so hungry for Him. Hegge prayed for God to come into his heart, forgive him of his sins, and to change his life forever. Not only did that happen, but his body was healed of tuberculosis as well!

Anna praised God for yet another showing of His divine intervention and mercy. She continued to claim victories for the rest of her family.

Hegge went on to found Burden Bearers, a Christian organization in Seattle, Washington offering counseling services to those with problems in their marriage, family difficulties, and personal problems of any kind. They also provided adoption services.

Using his Mother's concepts, Hegge saw God's miraculous healing of homosexuals, alcoholics and prostitutes. He saw marriages mended, divorce proceedings cancelled, and people brought to Christ.

No more information was found on Burden Bearers locally. When they were here, however, they did a great service to the local community. The family told me that Hegge's son is carrying on the legacy of Christian counseling in Chicago still today. There are also various branches throughout the country.

Hegge was a minister for 18 years as well as running Burden Bearers for over 30 years.

Anna's Crisis

One night, while on her way to a revival service in Olympia, the car that Anna was in hit a tree trunk and overturned on the highway between Yelm and Olympia at about the point where the Red Wind Casino now stands. Anna was very badly injured. Her right hand was caught under the side of the car and was totally mangled, requiring extensive surgery to repair and make it somewhat useful again. She was in surgery for many hours, loosing three fingers and about half of her palm.

Carl refused to visit her in the hospital saying he wouldn't go. He said to let the church take care of her, she wouldn't be any good to him any more, and she should just die. He had trouble understanding the reason why, of all the people in the car that night, his wife was the only one injured. The bottom line was that he needed her and he was afraid. The only way he knew to express his deepest fears was through anger and rage.

After Anna's surgery, during recuperation process, gangrene set in. Medicine of those days was much more barbaric. There wasn't anything the doctors could do but wait and see what happened. Anna was very frail and weak; her body couldn't take much more. She again did what she knew best and prayed. Anna was eventually released from the hospital and sent back to the farm. She lived through that terrible accident and surgery only to come home to a not-so-warm welcome from her husband.

Carl's reaction to Anna's return was, *"What good are you to me now? You can't milk the cows! You can't pick berries! You should have just died!"* Anna simply prayed again, "Lord, please give my hand the ability to milk these cows and pick these berries so that I may please Carl and please you." Amazingly, even with a badly disfigured right hand, Anna was able to do just that!

Anna's faith was so very strong. She would often pray for the animals on the farm when they became sick, and they all eventually got well. She prayed for the laboring animal mothers, and their young were always born into this world healthy. She prayed for the berries in the fields, and harvests were always plenty.

Many people, including her minister, told Anna that she

should leave Carl because he treated her so badly all of the time. Her faith, however, told her differently. Anna's faith was incredible in every possible way, and I have to admit, I highly admire it. She was the most Godly of women according to her eldest son.

1940–1950

From 1937 through 1942, Cam Iverson worked at Washington Veneer Company in Olympia, Washington. He was an off-bearer on a Veneer clipper for about a year and did various other jobs in the veneer field while he was there.

For those of you, like me, who don't know what veneer is or what an off-bearer does, I found some simple explanations that helped.

"Veneer is a thin leaf of wood applied with glue to a panel or frame of solid wood. The art of veneer developed with early civilization. It produces richly grained effects cheaply and is used also on structural parts that must be cut with the grain for strength. The grain pattern varies with the direction of the cut, woods cut across the grain in general displaying more effective patterns, e.g., burr and oyster walnut, bird's-eye maple. Rosewood, satinwood, maple, walnut, and mahogany are frequently employed for veneers. Hand-cut veneers were 1/10 to 1/8 in. thick; the modern machine-cut sheets are rarely thicker than 1/32 in. Veneering executed in inlaid sheets is known as marquetry. Plywood and beams or planks of compounded woods are developed by a veneering process." (Columbia Encyclopedia)

The off-bearer is the person that operates a huge band saw making the first rough cut on logs as they come into the mill. The saw sections off slices of wood that will later be cut into standard lengths and be planed for finished lumber. The position of an off-bearer is said to be one of the most dangerous jobs in the mill, and trust me, I read about some very horrendous accidents. Washington Veneer Company is no longer in business and therefore couldn't offer me any more information about Cam's personal service, but from what I have learned of him, it must have been good.

On January 16, 1942, Cam enlisted in the United States

Air Force out of Seattle, Washington. He was placed with the 8th Air Force, 79th Fighter Squadron. His military occupation was as a Cook, preparing food for a company mess hall, baking pies and pastries, rolls, etc. He also did meat cutting, quartering, finer cuts, and boning. He attended the Cooks and Bakers School at Camp Presidio in California for eight weeks to learn the tricks of his trade. From what I could find out, it was later named the Quartermaster Food Service School.

Cam, 1942

During WW II, Cam Iverson was stationed at King's Cliffe in England. King's Cliffe is an ancient stone village that thrives today with many small businesses; a post office, bakery, grocery store, pub, art gallery, several design studios, etc.

While enlisted, Cam participated in the Air Offensive, Europe; Ardennes Central Europe; Normandy; Northern France; Rhineland; Per Go 33 WD 45. He received a Good Conduct

Medal, European African Middle Eastern Service Medal, and a Distinguished Unit Badge. Cam spent exactly 1 year, 7 months, and 14 days stateside and 2 years, 1 month, and 27 days overseas during his entire service. The highest rank he ever held was Sergeant. I can tell you, he was very proud of that.

I contacted the historian for the 20th Fighter Wing Association, Mr. Arthur Sevigny. He was very helpful in tracking down information regarding Cam's particular unit and some of their history. I was able to borrow their history book, *"King's Cliffe - The 20th Fighter Group and the 446th. Air Group In the European Theater of Operations"*

The information gathered from those two sources is below.

In late 1942 Cam's unit moved from Paine Field in Seattle, Washington, to March Field in California. On August 11, 1943, they boarded a train and traveled across the country to Standish, Massachusetts. This was the European staging area. From there, the members of the 20th boarded the Queen Mary for a not-so-luxurious voyage across the seas.

The ship had been refurbished from a first class vacation vessel to accommodate more than 19,000 men. Rooms that had typically held two or three people were now holding 20 to 30 bunks double and triple stacked for both officers and enlisted personnel.

The trip overseas was an uneventful one, except for the constant drills and meals. The Units arrived at the Firth of Clyde on August 25, 1943, on the southwestern coast of Scotland. This "Firth" empties into the North Channel and is a long narrow estuary, which is also known as the wide part of a river where it nears the sea, consisting of both a fresh and salt-water mix.

From there they were taken to Greenock, Scotland and then on to their quarters at King's Cliffe Airfield, North Hamptonshire, England.

As I scanned through the pictures of various members of Cam's unit, I saw everyday people; grandfathers, fathers, uncles, nephews, brothers, and sons. It really made me think about just how much we sacrifice for this country of ours. With the current war going on in Iraq, and the instability of the universe as a whole, it makes me wonder why so many men and women do. My younger brother has been serving in the Air Force for many years now, so it really hit home for me.

Most of the stories I read were about courageous battles and lucky breaks. It must have been quite the adventure for sure. There were two pictures of Cam in the book, one was taken with the other cooks of his unit and another was of him holding a Thanksgiving turkey in 1944.

I have included below some segments from an Internet message board regarding wartime memories. Permission was given by the original authors to include them in this writing.

This will give you an idea of what life was like for the average person during World War II directly from their perspectives. These particular people were just children at the time of this war. They are written from a child's eye in an adult perspective, if that makes sense. I was able to understand the emotions they were going through.

From: "john hilliard"
To: "Laura M. Porras"
Subject: Re: War Memories
Date: Monday, February 23, 2004 5:52 AM

Hello Laura, Thank you for your very nice message regarding life in wartime England etc. please feel free to use any of my writings I would be very happy to know that it may be in any way educative or enlightening to someone. Please feel free to ask me at any time about those years, I could also put you in touch with others who, as children, both enjoyed some aspects of wartime life and also suffered badly. Kind regards to you. John Hilliard.

Below is John's recollection of those times.

Name: John Hilliard
Visited: Sun Feb 1 11:23:07 2004

Comments:

*I have included some of my experiences as an evac-
uee. There is so much that could be written, the blitz,
the incessant sirens at night or day on the way to
school, in school. Being in air raid shelters, wearing
gas masks, Mickey Mouse ones or otherwise. Being
in the underground tube station as a shelter, seeing
barrage balloons, seeing the enemy bombers glint-
ing in the searchlights beams, hearing the bombs
descending, hearing the anti-aircraft guns going off
and the shell exploding way up high.*

*Seeing the v1 doodle bugs going over and watching
as one ceased flight and dove down to massive explosion, (it fell into Lees road Hillingdon and demol-
ished pensioners home killing them both.)*

*Rationing of food, being given a tin of Cocoa pow-
der at school as a special wartime treat. I have often
wondered how many times some of us must have
heard the Sirens.*

*Recently I visited my old junior school in Hillingdon
heath and they still had wartime diary, the school secretary kindly gave me a copy. I counted the number
of times that lessons were stopped due to sirens going
off. During the quite period, 1943–45, it was about
80 and only during school hours, I must have heard
them many hundreds of times all together including
the time when I lived in SE5 area of London. No won-*

der then that some of us get a nasty feeling when one still hears the occasional siren go!!

From: "tony BLACKBURN"
To: "Laura M. Porras"
Subject: Re: War time memories
Date: Friday, February 20, 2004 8:39 AM

Hello Laura,

What a surprise to see your message. Of course you may use my memories. I would be more than glad for you to do so. I think my parent's generation was probably the last of the true stalwarts and can never thank them enough for what they did for us.

I wish you every success with your book and if there is anything I might expand on let me know.

Best Wishes,

Tony Blackburn

Below is Tony's account as it was originally written of life during that time.

Name: Tony Blackburn
Visited: Fri Aug 1 14:21:55 2003

Comments:

I was a war child. I was born in 1938 and lived on the outskirts of Liverpool throughout the war. We had an Anderson shelter in the garden and I can clearly remember being dressed in my siren suit and taken down to the shelter and hearing the sound of the German aircraft and the thump of the nearby ack-ack guns taking them on.

Had all the war time privations, no sweets, never had an orange or a banana until I was about 7 years old, no chocolate and I remember helping my mother bring home the rations. I remember children at school who we all had to pray for because they had lost their fathers, mostly in the merchant navy.

Did the usual things like collecting shrapnel from the ack-ack guns and seeing aircraft fuselages being transported from Liverpool docks to somewhere or other. We had a black American regiment stationed near us and we used to look at them in wonder. They were very kind and threw us chewing gum over the school hedge.

I remember the celebrations of VE Night and VJ Night and wondered why my mother and other women were crying. My father was a policeman all during the war and he would sometimes be able to pop in if there was a bad Liverpool blitz just to see we were OK.

My mother and father are now both dead but I only realized in later life what they had gone through and how they must have worried for me and my brother and sister. We owe their generation a massive debt and if this site perpetuates their memory then it serves a truly wonderful purpose. God bless them and all those who never saw the end of it.

Some of Cam's Unit

35

While in England, Cam met Gladys Smith.

Gladys Smith

Gladys was helping the Pastor's wife scrub the floor at The Assembly of God Church in Peterborough, England during the "black out" time, meaning that there was black curtain around the door. One Friday night, Cam and another American serviceman came around these black curtains asking what time services started. They were members of the Assembly of God Church here in Yelm and wanted to continue their worship. The Pastor's wife answered their questions.

Cam got a few of the other boys wrangled up and they all started attending, since the church was only eight miles from the base that they were stationed at. He was coming to services every Sunday morning and Gladys appreciated that this American Serviceman was so devoted to his faith during such questionable and traumatic times. It got so that Cam was eventually taking Gladys home after the services. He would stay the night and catch a ride back to the base the following morning. They were immediately smitten. One thing led to another and they were soon considered an item. They courted for 2 ½ years before he finally proposed to her.

Cam & Gladys

They were married on February 27, 1945 in Peterborough, England.

February 27, 1945

Wedding Party

Cam was able to return to Yelm directly after the war ended

in 1945 and the Military shipped all the Americans back. Gladys had to wait until February of 1946 to come overseas. There were several thousand other "War Brides" in the same situation. Many of them came to America on the same ships together.

During WWII more than 30,000 British War Brides were transported to the U.S. on various ocean liners. Brides came from over 50 countries. It is estimated that the US Population increased by more than 70,000 in early 1946.

Cam received his honorable discharge from the United States Air Force on October 26, 1945, at the convenience of the government. His unit was demobilized at the end of 1944. His full time in the service was 3 years, 9 months, and 11 days.

Following is a collection of official military paperwork regarding Cam Iverson's service.

KK					R
ENLISTED RECORD AND REPORT OF SEPARATION					
HONORABLE DISCHARGE					

1. LAST NAME - FIRST NAME - MIDDLE INITIAL	2. ARMY SERIAL NO.	3. GRADE	4. ARM OF SERVICE	5. COMPONENT
IVERSON CAMPBELL	19 074 657	SGT	AAF	AUS

6. ORGANIZATION	7. DATE OF SEPARATION	8. PLACE OF SEPARATION
79TH F SQ	26 OCT 45	SEPARATION CENTER FORT LEWIS WASH

9. PERMANENT ADDRESS FOR MAILING PURPOSES	10. DATE OF BIRTH	11. PLACE OF BIRTH
RT 1 BOX 220 YELM WASHINGTON	12 DEC 13	BUCHANNON CANADA

12. ADDRESS FROM WHICH EMPLOYMENT WILL BE SOUGHT	13. COLOR EYES	14. COLOR HAIR	15. HEIGHT	16. WEIGHT	17. NO. DEPEND.
SEE 9	BLUE	BLONDE	5' 9"	200 lbs	1

18. RACE	19.	20. U.S. CITIZEN	21. CIVILIAN OCCUPATION AND NO.
X	X	X	VENEER LEVERMAN-

MILITARY HISTORY

22. DATE OF INDUCTION	23. DATE OF ENLISTMENT	24. DATE OF ENTERING ACTIVE SERVICE	25. PLACE OF ENTRY INTO SERVICE
	16 JAN 42	16 JAN 42	SEATTLE WASH

26.	27.	28. COUNTY AND STATE	31. HOME ADDRESS AT TIME OF ENTRY INTO SERVICE
X			SEE 9

30. MILITARY OCCUPATIONAL SPECIALTY AND NO.	31. MILITARY QUALIFICATION
COOK 060	NONE

32. BATTLES AND CAMPAIGNS
AIR OFFENSIVE EUROPE ARDENNES CENTRAL EUROPE NORMANDY NORTHERN FRANCE RHINELAND PER GO 33 WD 45

33. DECORATIONS AND CITATIONS
GOOD CONDUCT MEDAL EUROPEAN AFRICAN MIDDLE EASTERN SERVICE MEDAL DISTINGUISHED UNIT BADGE GO 34 WD 45

34. WOUNDS RECEIVED IN ACTION
NONE

35. LATEST IMMUNIZATION DATES				36. SERVICE OUTSIDE CONTINENTAL U.S. AND RETURN		
SMALLPOX	TYPHOID	TETANUS	OTHER (specify)	DATE OF DEPARTURE	DESTINATION	DATE OF ARRIVAL
MAR 44	AUG 45	OCT 42	TYPH AUG 45	20 AUG 43	E A M E	26 AUG 43
				11 OCT 45	U S	16 OCT 45

37. TOTAL LENGTH OF SERVICE				38. HIGHEST GRADE HELD
CONTINENTAL SERVICE		FOREIGN SERVICE		SGT
YEARS	MONTHS	DAYS	YEARS	MONTHS	DAYS
1	7	14	2	1	27

39. PRIOR SERVICE
NONE

40. REASON AND AUTHORITY FOR SEPARATION
CONVENIENCE OF GOVERNMENT RR 1-1 "DEMOBILIZATION" AR 615-365 15 DEC 44

41. SERVICE SCHOOLS ATTENDED	42. EDUCATION (Years)		
QM COOKS & BAKERS	Grammar	High School	College
	8	0	0

PAY DATA

43. LONGEVITY FOR PAY PURPOSES	44. MUSTERING OUT PAY	45. SOLDIER DEPOSIT	46. TRAVEL PAY	47. TOTAL AMOUNT, NAME OF DISBURSING OFFICER
YEARS	MONTHS	DAYS	TOTAL	THIS PAYMENT			
3	9	11	$300	$100	none	$80	180 80 E W WOHLGEMUTH CAPT FD

INSURANCE NOTICE

48. KIND OF INSURANCE	49. HOW PAID	50. EFFECTIVE DATE OF ALLOT.	51. DATE OF NEXT PREMIUM DUE	52. PREMIUM DUE	53. INTENTION OF VETERAN TO
X	X	31 OCT 45	30 NOV 45	$7 20	X

54.	53. REMARKS
	LAPEL BUTTON ISSUED ASR SCORE (2 SEP 45) 99

RIGHT THUMB PRINT

56. SIGNATURE OF PERSON BEING SEPARATED	57. PERSONNEL OFFICER (Type name, grade and organization - signature)
Campbell I Iverson	JOHN J TAGGART MAJOR AGD *John J Taggart*

WD AGO FORM 53-55
1 November 1944

This form supersedes all previous editions of WD AGO Forms 53 and 55 for enlisted persons entitled to an Honorable Discharge, which will not be used after receipt of this revision.

Honorable Discharge

This is to certify that

CAMPBELL IVERSON 19 074 657 SERGEANT

79TH FTR SQ

Army of the United States

is hereby Honorably Discharged from the military service of the United States of America.

This certificate is awarded as a testimonial of Honest and Faithful Service to this country.

Given at SEPARATION CENTER
FORT LEWIS WASHINGTON

Date 26 OCTOBER 1945

Harvey D. Taylor
HARVEY D TAYLOR
LIEUTENANT COLONEL CAVALRY

Cam's Discharge Papers

KK

Army of the United States

SEPARATION QUALIFICATION RECORD
SAVE THIS FORM. IT WILL NOT BE REPLACED IF LOST

This record of job assignments and special training received in the Army is furnished to the soldier when he leaves the service. In its preparation, information is taken from available Army records and supplemented by personal interview. The information about civilian education and work experience is based on the individual's own statements. The veteran may present this document to former employers, prospective employers, representatives of schools or colleges, or use it in any other way that may prove beneficial to him.

1. LAST NAME—FIRST NAME—MIDDLE INITIAL				MILITARY OCCUPATIONAL ASSIGNMENTS			
IVERSON, CAMPBELL				10. MONTHS	11. GRADE	12. MILITARY OCCUPATIONAL SPECIALTY	
2. ARMY SERIAL NO.	3. GRADE	4. SOCIAL SECURITY NO.		39	Sgt	Cook	060
19 074 657	Sgt	535-10-3438					
5. PERMANENT MAILING ADDRESS (Street, City, County, State)							
Rt 1, Box 220 Yelm, Thurstone Co, Washington							
6. DATE OF ENTRY INTO ACTIVE SERVICE	7. DATE OF SEPARATION	8. DATE OF BIRTH					
16 Jan 42	26 Oct 45	12 Dec 13					
9. PLACE OF SEPARATION							
Separation Center, Ft. Lewis, Washington							

SUMMARY OF MILITARY OCCUPATIONS

13. TITLE—DESCRIPTION—

COOK--Prepared food for a company mess hall. Baked pies, pasteries, rolls, etc. Did meat cutting, quartered, made finer cuts, boned.

WD AGO FORM 100 BFW
1 JUL 1945

This form supersedes WD AGO Form 100, 15 July 1944, which will not be used.

16—43815-1

42

LAURA M. PORRAS

MILITARY EDUCATION

14. NAME OR TYPE OF SCHOOL—COURSE OR CURRICULUM—DURATION—DESCRIPTION

Cooks and Bakers School, Camp Presidio, California; Cooking and Baking; 8 weeks.

CIVILIAN EDUCATION

15. HIGHEST GRADE COMPLETED	16. DEGREES OR DIPLOMAS	17. YEAR LEFT SCHOOL	OTHER TRAINING OR SCHOOLING	
			20. COURSE—NAME AND ADDRESS OF SCHOOL—DATE	21. DURATION
8	Graduated	1927	None	

18. NAME AND ADDRESS OF LAST SCHOOL ATTENDED

Yelm, Washington

19. MAJOR COURSES OF STUDY

None

CIVILIAN OCCUPATIONS

22. TITLE—NAME AND ADDRESS OF EMPLOYER—INCLUSIVE DATES—DESCRIPTION

VENEER LEVERMAN--Operated machine that stacked sheeted lumber for 5 years (1937-42) for Washington Veneer Co, Olympia Washington. Was off bearer on clipper for about a year, and did various other jobs in veneer work.

ADDITIONAL INFORMATION

23. REMARKS

24. SIGNATURE OF PERSON BEING SEPARATED	25. SIGNATURE OF SEPARATION CLASSIFICATION OFFICER	26. NAME OF OFFICER (Typed or Stamped)
	Hugh K Marshall	HUGH K. MARSHALL, Capt. MAC

☆ U. S. GOVERNMENT PRINTING OFFICE   16—45815-1

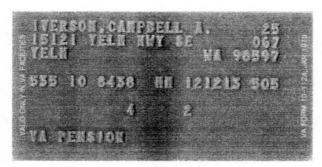

Cam's Dog Tag

Cam's Veteran's Registration

Unfortunately, the official records that I requested directly from the US Government were not available due to a nasty little fire they had back in the 70's.

LAURA M. PORRAS

 National Personnel Records Center

Military Personnel Records, *9700 Page Avenue St. Louis, Missouri 63132-5100*

July 5, 2004

Laura Porras
18124 Sundown Court SE
Yelm, WA 98597

RE: Veteran's Name: **IVERSON CAMPBELL**
         SSN/SN: **535108438/19074657**
         Request Number: **1-98802404**

Dear Sir or Madam:

The record needed to answer your inquiry is not in our files. If the record were here on July 12, 1973, it would have been in the area that suffered the most damage in the fire on that date and may have been destroyed. The fire destroyed the major portion of records of Army military personnel for the period 1912 through 1959, and records of Air Force personnel with surnames Hubbard through Z for the period 1947 through 1963. Fortunately, there are alternate records sources that often contain information which can be used to reconstruct service record data lost in the fire; however, complete personnel/medical records cannot be reconstructed.

We are pleased to enclose NA Form 13038, *Certification of Military Service*. This document verifies military service and may be used for any official purpose. A seal has been affixed to this document to attest to its authenticity. The information used to prepare the enclosed NA Form 13038 was obtained from an alternate record source.

If you have questions or comments regarding this response, you may contact us at 314-801-0800 or by mail at the address shown in the letterhead above. If you contact us, please reference the Request Number listed above. If you are a veteran, or a deceased veteran's next of kin, please consider submitting your future requests online by visiting us at http://vetrecs.archives.gov.

Sincerely,

J. HARRIS
Archives Technician (5B)

Enclosure(s)

ENLISTED RECORD AND REPORT OF SEPARATION
HONORABLE DISCHARGE

VOL 3 PAGE 388

1. LAST NAME - FIRST NAME - MIDDLE INITIAL: IVERSON CAMPBELL
2. ARMY SERIAL NO.: 19 074 657
3. GRADE: SGT
4. ARM OR SERVICE: AAF
5. COMPONENT: AUS
6. ORGANIZATION: 79TH F SQ
7. DATE OF SEPARATION: 26 OCT 45
8. PLACE OF SEPARATION: SEPARATION CENTER FORT LEWIS WASH
9. PERMANENT ADDRESS FOR MAILING PURPOSES: RT 1 BOX 220 YELM WASHINGTON
10. DATE OF BIRTH: 12 DEC 13
11. PLACE OF BIRTH: BUCHANNON CANADA
12. ADDRESS FROM WHICH EMPLOYMENT WILL BE SOUGHT: SEE 9
13. COLOR EYES: BLUE 14. COLOR HAIR: BLONDE 15. HEIGHT: 5' 9" 16. WEIGHT: 200 LBS
18. RACE: WHITE X 19. MARITAL STATUS: MARRIED X 20. U.S. CITIZEN: YES X
21. CIVILIAN OCCUPATION AND NO.: VENEER LEVERMAN

MILITARY HISTORY

22. DATE OF INDUCTION: 16 JAN 42
24. DATE OF ENTRY INTO ACTIVE SERVICE: 16 JAN 42
25. PLACE OF ENTRY INTO SERVICE: SEATTLE WASH
29. HOME ADDRESS AT TIME OF ENTRY INTO SERVICE: SEE 9
26. REGISTERED X
30. MILITARY OCCUPATIONAL SPECIALTY AND NO.: COOK 060
31. MILITARY QUALIFICATION AND DATE: NONE
32. BATTLES AND CAMPAIGNS: AIR OFFENSIVE EUROPE ARDENNES CENTRAL EUROPE NORMANDY NORTHERN FRANCE RHINELAND PER GO 33 WD 45
33. DECORATIONS AND CITATIONS: GOOD CONDUCT MEDAL EUROPEAN AFRICAN MIDDLE EASTERN SERVICE MEDAL DISTINGUISHED UNIT BADGE GO 34 WD 45
34. WOUNDS RECEIVED IN ACTION: NONE

35. LATEST IMMUNIZATION DATES: SMALLPOX MAR 44 TYPHOID AUG 45 TETANUS OCT 42 OTHER (specify) TYPH AUG 45
36. DATE OF DEPARTURE: 20 AUG 43 DESTINATION: E A M E DATE OF ARRIVAL: 26 AUG 43
37. TOTAL LENGTH OF SERVICE: CONTINENTAL SERVICE YEARS 1 MONTHS 7 DAYS 14 FOREIGN SERVICE YEARS 2 MONTHS 1 DAYS 27
34. HIGHEST GRADE HELD: SGT
DATE OF DEPARTURE: 11 OCT 45 DESTINATION: U S DATE OF ARRIVAL: 16 OCT 45
38. PRIOR SERVICE: NONE

40. REASON AND AUTHORITY FOR SEPARATION: CONVENIENCE OF GOVERNMENT RR 1-1 "DEMOBILIZATION" AR 615-365 15 DEC 44
41. SERVICE SCHOOLS ATTENDED: QM COOKS & BAKERS
42. EDUCATION (Years): GRAMMAR SCHOOL 8 HIGH SCHOOL 0 COLLEGE 0

PAY DATA

43. LONGEVITY FOR PAY PURPOSES: YEARS 3 MONTHS 11
44. MUSTERING OUT PAY: TOTAL 300 THIS PAYMENT 100
45. SOLDIER DEPOSITED: non
46. TRAVEL PAY: 80
47. TOTAL AMOUNT, NAME OF DISBURSING OFFICER: 180 80 E W WOHLGEMUTH CAPT FD

INSURANCE NOTICE
48. KIND OF INSURANCE: Nat Serv X U.S. Govt.
49. HOW PAID: Allotment X
50. Effective Date of Allotment Discontinuance: 31 OCT 45
51. Date of Next Premium Due (One month after 50): 30 NOV 45
52. PREMIUM DUE EACH MONTH: 7 20
53. INTENTION OF VETERAN TO CONTINUE: X

55. REMARKS: LAPEL BUTTON ISSUED
ASR SCORE (2 SEP 45) 99

56. SIGNATURE OF PERSON BEING SEPARATED: Campbell A. Iverson
57. PERSONNEL OFFICER: JOHN J TAGGART MAJOR AGD

After Cam and Gladys were reunited in early 1945, they moved in with his folks in Yelm. He went back to work for Georgia Pacific and they settled into their normal domestic life. A few months later, they applied for a VA loan and bought a house of their own across from the local Assembly of God Church.

November 30, 1945 brought Cam and Gladys their first child, a son they named Michael.

Gladys, Cam & Michael

Followed on October 12, 1947 by their first daughter, Sharon.

Michael & Sharon

Anna stayed with Carl until the day she died.

With her final breath, her only concern was that her family was saved. The children, following her example, had all given themselves to Jesus, but Carl was holding back for unknown reasons; he could often be overheard saying, "I don't see Jesus answering your prayers." Anna always persisted, *"Papa, give your heart to Jesus!"* She pleaded with him, begged him. That is all she could say as she was lying on the kitchen floor having a stroke.

Papa was 80 years old when he finally did just that. He gave his heart to Jesus, and the whole family was saved.

Anna, at the age of 68, passed away due to heart complications and pneumonia at Tacoma General Hospital on October 6, 1947. She had been in the hospital for nine days. Cam was at his mother's side when she took her final breath. She said to him, "Beautiful music, lovely music." With a wonderful smile on her face, she was finally at peace.

Sharon, Cam's first daughter, was born six days later.

In Memory of Mom Iverson

By her daughter-in-law
Lillian Hill Iverson

I have a memory so sweet and so true
Of a dear godly mother of which there are few.
Her faith was so simple; her heart was so kind;
The people all loved her; her type's hard to find.
A precious black Bible in memory's view,
A small pair of glasses we find in it, too.
It's a symbol of what in her life counted most;
Dear God, may we follow, no matter what cost.
She was quiet and meek, yet held mighty sway
In the hearts of her children, and others who say
Her life was a message from God all His own;
We'd do well to pattern this guide to the Throne.
She wanted no credit for anything done;
Her only desire, praise for Jesus alone!
In her last conscious moments His name on her lips
In a challenge to all, lest our feet should e're slip.
We shall cherish forever this memory so real
And God grant our own lives shall to others appeal.

October 8, 1947

Love, Lillian Iverson

1950–1965

Within five years, Cam's mother had died and his father didn't want to live alone in a big house. Cam and Gladys sold their home close by and bought his parent's place on Yelm Avenue. Cam's Dad lived in a small trailer on the property until he died.

On August 20, 1951, Desmond was born to Gladys and Cam, he was their second son.

Cam's sister, Ruth, arrived in Tokyo in May of 1952 with her husband, Robert Frivold, and her two daughters. She went on to be a missionary in Japan for the next 30 plus years and had two sons. Anna's faith and vision had inspired Ruth to spiritual greatness. Ten thousand copies of Anna's testimony that Hegge wrote, "Mother's Wonder-Working Words," were distributed to the Japanese in their own language. One was even presented to Princess Michiko of the Royal Family!

Two and a half years after Desmond was born, Gladys gave birth to their third son Vernon, on January 19, 1954.

Carl passed away on October 3, 1957, nearly 10 years after Anna, due to complications of pneumonia and high blood pressure. He is buried in the Yelm Cemetery.

Gladys gave birth to their second daughter and youngest child, Darlene, on January 4, 1962.

Iverson Family

Cam had worked for Georgia Pacific Corporation before joining the service and returned there after coming home. It was one of the conditions of his enlistment that he was allowed to return to his original position. Approximately two years later he worked for the Western Farmers Co-op in Yelm. Cam was also a member of the Butcher Workman Union of Tacoma.

Cam as a Father

In my research I had many wonderful conversations with Cam's children. Every time his eldest daughter Sharon spoke of him, her face would light up, and she would get this glorious look of sincere admiration in her eyes. I can only pray that my own children admire me so much when I am gone! Sharon has part of a room in her home dedicated to the memory of her Dad. She keeps his pictures and many mementos in there.

Sharon recalls her father as a very loving and generous man. He always had time for her and they shared a very special father-daughter bond. She took on many of his more compassionate traits and makes herself available to her sons and grandchildren on a moment's notice, as well as to anyone else that is in need.

Cam's eldest son Michael inherited a slight speech impediment and, like Cam, doesn't let it get in his way. Michael recalls that the children were taught a lot of responsibility because of the farm. There were always chores to be done and plenty of hands to help out doing them. He also remembers tagging along many times while Cam helped others. He was amazed at his father's presence. Mike specifically remembers one incident when Cam was called to assist at a train wreck. Apparently some cows had been slaughtered and the owner called Cam in to salvage some of the meat! Cam was there to do his civic duty and make sure that the cows were treated humanely.

Mike's favorite memory of his Dad was of going to Lake Lawrence in the summer. Cam would lift his son onto his shoulders and throw him in the lake to teach him how to swim.

Cam and Gladys made so many sacrifices for their family over the years. Mike suffered from asthma and had to go to Seattle often for treatment. The gasoline alone for the trip would take up the whole milk fund for the month. Mike knew how much of a sacrifice that was for his health and well-being and was very grateful for it.

He, like Sharon, remembers that his Dad always made himself available for the important things. Mike had a paper route for seven years and Cam would take him around his route in the car when he was too sick to do it by himself.

The good news is that Mike eventually overcame his asthma as he followed in his father's footsteps and joined the military as a cook. The strenuous workouts and constant running helped to strengthen his lungs and he hasn't had any trouble with his breathing since.

Gladys always made sure that the kids ate a good nutritious meal each morning before leaving for school. These days we shove our kids out the door with a cereal bar in their hands and a quick kiss on the cheek.

Back then, Cam and Gladys provided a hot meal that always began with fresh fruit from their gardens. It was then followed with eggs, bacon, pancakes, and the like each and every day. The hot cereal they ate was called mush back then!

Mike told me that he didn't even know what cold cereal or pastry was until much later in life. He also recalled their family tradition of Sunday afternoon dinners together and holds these memories close.

1965–1985

One Monday evening in June of 1965, Cam was working around the house when suddenly he began having severe chest pains. This wasn't something he had experienced before so it was quite shocking when it happened. Cam came in the house holding his chest groaning. Everyone knew something was desperately wrong because he never complained about anything.

"I feel like an elephant is stepping on my chest," he said. Gladys called Dr. John McNamara and he rushed out to the house. In those days, house calls were still a common occurrence. Cam was rushed by ambulance to a hospital in Olympia for treatment.

On the way to the hospital, Cam made a vow to God. He said, "Lord, if you let me live, I will do anything you ask of me." He was in the hospital for an entire month. Gladys was left to tend to the children on her own. Their oldest was attending Centralia Junior College at the time and their youngest was still a toddler.

Shortly after Cam was released from the hospital, he went back to work. Soon there after, he suffered more chest pains and high blood pressure. The doctors told him he couldn't go back to his current occupation. Very reluctantly, he left his job and "retired" to taking care of the house.

With a son in college, a daughter in diapers, and a few in between, Cam was now faced with the question of how he was going to support his family. Options were limited, so he was forced to start collecting Social Security.

Country Community Chapel is Born

Denomination: a religious organization uniting local congregations in a single legal and administrative body

Non: not: other than: reverse of: absence of
Nondenominational: not: other than: reverse of: absence of a religious organization uniting local congregations in a single legal and administrative body

In 1968, Cam would take on his greatest personal challenge. Gladys received a phone call from some of the ladies at the McKenna Community Church, which was located in a small town two miles away. Today that very church has been converted into the Old Steeple Book store along the main highway between Roy and Yelm. Cam built the new addition that now holds its flower and gift shop.

The pastor of the McKenna Church had gone away, and they needed someone to fill his place temporarily. It was a very small congregation and they could only afford to pay $10 a week. The ladies wanted to know if Cam would take the job in the interim. Gladys suggested that they ask him to come, give his testimony and give a little talk until they could find another pastor to take his place. Cam had no formal religious training, only having served as a Deacon before. The ladies seemed happy with this option and asked Cam if he would do it. His response was, "Yes, I can do that."

Cam built a small chicken-incubating house, which he converted in to a prayer room after accepting the position of Pastor for the McKenna Community Church. Darlene had also wanted to use it as a dollhouse!

Cam's testimony was about his mother, his siblings, his life of sin, and turning that life around to live as a God-fearing Christian. Needless to say that after the 3rd Sunday the congregation as a whole wanted him as their Pastor full time.

Knowing what his answer would be, Edith Rogers told him to go home and pray about it. She was a very wise woman! Cam was about to say no, but instead went to his prayer room and had a talk with God. His argument was that he hadn't had any formal training, and he felt very uneducated, so there was no way he could accomplish what they were asking of him.

After praying, he remembered the promise he had made in the back of the ambulance that day in 1965. He knew that this was his calling and this was what the Lord wanted him to do. His life had been spared three years earlier for a reason.

The Lord answered Cam in saying, "Ye have not chosen me, but I have chosen you, and ordained you, that ye should go and bring forth fruit, and that your fruit should remain: that whatsoever ye shall ask of the Father in my name, he may give it you." John 5:16 (KJV)

Cam accepted the position. Every day he would go to his prayer room to seek guidance and write his sermons. Each one of those sermons was written out by hand. He never used a typewriter and didn't feel comfortable with "modern technology." He enjoyed his quiet time with the Lord on a daily basis, reading his Bible and studying the scriptures.

Not wanting to affect his social security income, he used the $10 a week they had offered, for gas money instead of pay. He knew that God would provide for him and his family as long as he followed His will.

Within 7-½ years, a congregation of 15–20 people, most of them women, had multiplied to more than 200. The church was full and they needed more space.

Friends gave Cam and Gladys some property on Morris Road in Yelm to build a new church. During the 4-½ years it took to build the church, services were held at the Middle School Classatorium.

Mother's Day 1977

Cam knew then what many of us today still fail to realize, that it all starts at home. His entire sermon that day was about the grace of mothers. Women should be devoted to their husbands and husbands to their wives. It has always been a two way street, we just forget that some times. When we stop caring for each other is when we truly fall from God's grace.

"Don't color your hair," Cam said, "leave it natural; you earned it!"

A good man that loves his wife will lend a hand around the house. "You are not too big to wash a dish," Cam said to the husbands in his congregation. He always enjoyed helping his wife in the kitchen.

Cam claimed all of his ministries and those of his siblings were his Mother's ministries through her children. Because of her faithfulness and devotion, they went on to do great things. If it were not for her, they wouldn't have been here and be who they were.

Anna went through hell for years so that her ministry would blossom out through them. She was only 68 when she died but she looked as if she were 98. In her relatively short life she had grown very frail. She had lived a life of obstacles, hardship, and adversity. Anna walked to church every Sunday and never missed a service. Her faith was that strong! She knew hard work and did it with a true joy in her heart. No one helped her around the house.

Cam stressed that these days it is different, we are all expected to do our part to make our lives work. If our lives are falling apart, we need to look within to find the answers.

Sermons And Ministry

Through listening to tapes of Cam's various sermons, I heard many of the same messages repeated time after time. It was all the same kind of fire and brimstone, but the point he was making was very clear. He felt that the Second Coming of The Lord was near and that we were not at all ready for it.

God is calling upon his people, many will be called but only a few will be chosen. What a man sows, he must also reap. Too many of us are mocking God in what we say and do and how we live our lives. It is not at all being taken lightly. God will be our ultimate judge. Cam said, "Don't you judge me; let

God be the one to do it." He stressed walking the straight and narrow path, making sure that you are right with God before that judgment day comes.

His sermons also stressed unity, integrity, morality, and spirituality. So many religious leaders of today are more concerned with financial affairs and worldly goods than of faith itself. We are backing away from the core values of the book that we all claim to believe in, the Bible.

Although some of the Bible can't be taken word for word literally, Cam did a fantastic job of bringing those messages and their meanings into modern terms. He used today's terminology while maintaining the core values within the original words. God's word is the same, yesterday, today, and tomorrow.

Cam also stressed focusing on the local church first. Being faithful to your church and acting as an advocate for Christianity was also a key point. The way you leave this world is the way in which you will stand before God. Other countries don't have the religious outlets that we do and we should be thankful. I would have really enjoyed being one of those sheep in his flock.

One other point I want to note is the concept of "speaking in tongues." I checked with Cam's grandson, Jon Bellows, Jr., and he said that this was a common occurrence within the church. I myself have never witnessed it, but I did hear it on several tapes I listened to.

Usually it was an individual in the background speaking loudly in a language that I couldn't comprehend and then someone else speaking in English, as if in translation. On one of the tapes, Cam himself did it. Sharon told me that he did this at almost all of his services. That is when I started researching the phenomenon to better understand it.

Although every denomination has their own view of the "gift," I was brought up to believe it had more evil roots than good. I was brought up Roman Catholic and had religion poured down my throat like a nasty tasting elixir. We all know that today's news is filled with the hypocrisy and crimes of the "men of cloth." For me personally, I choose to have faith without the bricks and mortar.

After researching this phenomenon, I have a much more liberal view on its validity. There are many places in the Bible that refer to "speaking in tongues" as a valid gift from God. Some say that it is a language spoken by angels or God Himself and that it is not similar to anything in the human vernacular. It was a frequent occurrence many centuries ago and has only recently been made popular again.

Believers in this "gift" began to speak in other languages that even they didn't understand. The result, according to the Bible, is that many people passing by can hear the gospel in their native language. They usually became convicted by the message they heard and became instant believers in Jesus. It is clearly stated in 1 Corinthians 14, that the specific purpose is conversion of non-believers and that there should be someone to interpret what has been said. Knowing that, I now understand what I was hearing.

I also read that this practice specifically does not include women. Being a woman, I personally take offense, but only for a moment. I have no desire to speak in any other language than my own right now. I still don't truly understand why women are not "allowed" to speak in tongues.

Cam however, did allow the women of his congregation to practice this occurrence. There weren't many men in the church at the time. To solve this problem, the Saturday night before, Cam would oftentimes be found anointing the pews. He would pray for the families of his congregation in order to bring more people into his little church.

Cam had very specific thoughts on a woman's place in the church and that was not anywhere near a pulpit. This is also stated in the Bible itself, but as we all know, there are just as many female religious leaders these days as there are male.

I wonder if any of them have read the same passages I did. "But I suffer not a woman to teach, nor to usurp authority over the man, but to be in silence" (1 Timothy 2: 12). Simply stated, she may pray, teach and testify, to other women and children, she just can't have more authority than the men.

The bottom line is that my research led me to a different view than that of which I was raised. I now see speaking in tongues as a unique ability given to those with spiritual blessings. Apparently Cam was one of those gifted few. I can only imagine the feelings he had when these gifts came to him. How powerful they must have been!

I was told by members of his church that quite a few mothers went to him asking for prayers over the years. When they were unable to conceive and all else had failed, Cam would do what he did best and he prayed for them.

Would you believe that each and every one of those mothers had healthy beautiful babies after that? It was the same with sick animals on the various farmlands around here. Cam would pray for them and miraculously they would all recover from their various ailments. He also used the same handkerchief anointing that I mentioned earlier regarding Anna's abscess.

Cam loved his three gardens that he had affectionately named, Spring, Summer, and Fall. He could oftentimes be found outside milling around in them, formulating many of his sermons as he was on his hands and knees weeding. The Iversons raised raspberries commercially for their main income. At that time they charged $2.50 a flat! (If only!) As Cam was out in the fields picking berries one day, the name for his new church suddenly came to him; Country Community Chapel. He knew immediately that was what it should be called.

The dedication ceremony for the new church was held on November 16, 1980. It was a very musical celebration and there wasn't a dry eye in the place. Cam said a beautiful opening prayer and everyone broke out into song again. He was very touched with the number of people from every location, denomination, and background that were there. I could hear the tears in his voice while listening to the tape of the service. He was so proud of his flock! Several other Pastors also came to join in the celebration.

The Mayor of Yelm at the time, Lora B. Coates, was asked to come forward and share with the community. She was very emotional and could only say, "God Bless you all!"

Cam was sure to make special mention of Brother Dan Cook, the man that was an integral part of his salvation. He felt that Brother Cook would be at the top of God's list one day. He was the founder of The Assembly of God Church in Yelm and he was a leader both in everyday life and in his Church. In a few days, on Thanksgiving of 1980, he was turning 93 years old, but Cam noted that his spirit was still very strong.

1980

Pastor's Perspective

Let's Renew Our Commitment
By CAMPBELL IVERSON
Yelm Country Community Chapel

Proverbs 14:34 (KJV): "Righteousness exalted a nation: but sin is a reproach to any people."

As a pastor of a lovely, growing church, I am very deeply concerned about our homes that are crumbling and falling apart all around us. Last year, Thurston County had more divorces than marriages, and our adjoining counties reported same.

Our home is a God-given institution, and God has laid out a beautiful plan for its maintenance and upkeep. If we will follow God's divine plan, every home can be a blessing and a great success.

Successful and Godly homes give us a strong commu-nity, strong local churches. It helps to develop strong, healthy and spiritual young people. The destruction of our homes causes our nation to weaken and crumble. The effects of it have already been felt in every community.

If we, who are called Christians, don't help stem this damaging and destructful task, we are in for grave trouble. God has given every home the key. This master key is "righteousness." It will exalt (lift up) or build a nation, community, homes, and last, but not least, the most important—the individual.

A true quotation has been said: "The family that prays together, stays together." This world is hard, cruel and very black. Without divine guidance and obedience to God's divine plan, we are no match for the destroyer, who is Satan.

Let's build, or if our structure has crumbled, let's renew the structure of the home on the one and only true foundation which has already been laid, who is a person, and His name is Jesus, our lovely Christ.

Let's renew our strength, commitment and faith to the one and only one who cannot only make a home but will maintain it. Invite the Lord of the Universe to come on the scene, let Him call all the signals, execute His commands and your home will become a blessing. Dad and mom, you'll be fun to live with and your children will rise up and call you "blessed."

We read in the papers and hear on the air
Of killing and stealing and crime everywhere.
We sigh and say, as we notice the trend,
"This young generation . . . Where will it end?"
But can we be sure that it's their fault alone?
Are we less guilty, who place in their way;

A PROMISE TO GOD

Too many things that lead them astray?
Too much money, too much idle time;
Too many movies of passion and crime.
Too many books not fit to be read;
Too much evil in what they hear said.
Too many children encouraged to roam;
Too many parents who won't stay at home.
Kids don't make the movies,
they don't write the books;
They don't paint gay pictures of gangsters and
crooks.
They don't make the liquor, they don't run the bars;
They don't make the laws, and they don't make the
cars.
They don't peddle the drugs that muddle the brain;
That's all done by older folks, greedy for gain.
Delinquent teenagers—oh, how we condemn
For the sins of the nation, and blame it on them.
By the laws of the blameless, the Saviour made
known:
Who is there among us to cast the first stone?
For in so many cases—it's said but it's true,
The title "delinquent" fits older folks, too.

Saturday, July 21, 1984

Liquor's evil cannot be overestimated
By CAMPBELL IVERSON
Country Community Chapel
Pastor's Perspective

My subject won't be too well received by some; but regardless of whom it affects, it remains a very serious issue in our way of life. It's having a devastating effect upon our country and society, even our churches.

This issue is our "liquor traffic."

I am a sworn, eternal, uncompromising enemy of its use. It's one of the greatest killers in our society. There are more deaths contributed directly and indirectly to the use of alcohol than any other avenue in our lovely country. This killer has no mercy; it affects the poor and rich.

It has reached to an epidemic proportion in our school, with an explosion of teenage alcoholics, and they are our leaders of tomorrow. Fornication, adultery and homosexuality are running rampant on account of it.

The archbishop said, "I find social crime and ask, what's the greatest cause? (drinks); I find poverty, what's the greatest cause? (drinks); I find broken homes, and the greatest cause is drinks. I stand behind the scaffold and ask, what makes you a murderer? They cry, drinks."

This killer is more destructive than war, pestilence and famine. It's a living cancer in our human society, literally eating out its vitals and threatening our country's destruction. This deadly avenue tends to produce idleness, disease, pauperism and crime. A United States Supreme Court Judge said, "After 40 years at the bar and 10 years as a judge, I have no hesitancy in saying that 90 percent of the crime is related to alcohol."

Who foots the bills? The landlord who loses his rent, the baker, butcher and grocer whose goods the drunkard needs. The charitable people who pity the children dig deep in their pockets to keep them from going hungry.

The taxpayers have to support bigger and better institutions that this deadly killer keeps filled to overflowing. Our alms houses and reformatories are crowded to capacity. What's the greatest cause? Alcohol. Who makes the money? The breweries, distillers and saloon keepers. Who helps to fill this land with poverty, wretchedness, madness, crime, diseases, damnation and death?

We could build several million homes for the low-income people with the money that is spent in booze yearly.

Our insurance rates have reached a staggering high on everything. Why? Because of the unsafe society we live in. And still after all this, we as pastors and Christian laity are silent on this issue of death and destruction.

We view the wine and beer ads on TV, and they use an attractive model for their commercials. But they never film a poor, sick broken mother who has to live on welfare while her husband is sitting at the bar. Does it make sense?

Another disturbing factor to me is that each community gives a report at the end of the year how much revenue this deadly killer has contributed to the town coffers and government, not declaring or reporting how much it costs the local taxpayers for the devastating effects of death, destruction, disorder, vandalism and robbery.

I could write a book on this monster killer that's affecting every man, woman and child. I feel very strongly as a local pastor that we are authorized and commanded by God to "blow the trumpet loud and clear." We may lose some financial supporters, popularity and be ridiculed, but this is the price we must pay to find favor with God and his blessings.

Before I met my lovely Christ 44 years ago, my life was shambles and almost un-mend-able on account of alcohol. So I can pen this article with living, tangible proof of its deadly effects. Spiritual leaders, stand up and be counted, blow the trumpet loud and clear, and God's blessing and favor will be yours.

Two scriptures in closing:

"Wine is a mocker; strong drink is raging; and whosoever is deceived thereby is not wise." (Proverbs 20:1 KJV)

"Who hath woe? Who hath sorrow? Who hath redness of eyes? They that tarry long at the wine, they that go to seek mixed wine. Look not thou upon the wine when it is red, when it giveth his color in the cup, when it moveth itself aright. At the last it biteth like a serpent and stingeth like an adder." (Proverbs 23:29–32 KJV)

Adeline Comes a Little Closer

Adeline was a wonderful wife and mother; however, she scoffed the Lord and refused to believe that all of the miracles taking place in their home were His working. It wasn't until Cam came to her at the end of her life and they prayed together that she gave her life to Jesus.

She had smoked profusely for more than 40 years and was an alcoholic, as was her husband, John. Her body and soul became riddled by the sins of the flesh. Many times she had tried to quit, and many times she had not been able to.

Knowing that his sister was near the end of her time on this earth, Cam couldn't sleep one night. He had Adeline on his mind and prayed, "Lord, I want to get that girl and reinstate her back to Christ!" Cam really wanted to be sure that she went in the right order, being in the right place in her heart and soul. He said to Gladys, "Honey, I gotta go in the morning, I am desperate for her soul!" The next morning he went to visit Adeline at home.

"What brings you here so early Cam, is there something wrong?"

"Why, yes there is."

"What's the matter?"

"Well Adeline, I am concerned about you."

"What are you concerned about me for?"

"Well, Adeline, we had a precious Mother who always claimed her family for God, and this morning, I am not too certain whether the security with you is there. How is it, Adeline? If you should be taken home, is everything all right?"

"Cam, it isn't as close as I would like to have it."

"What do you say we make it a little closer?"

"All right."

So they gathered together and joined hands. That morning Adeline dedicated her life to Jesus Christ. She said, "Lord, take my life and help me to be intimately related the way that I should be." The last member of the family had finally dedicated her life to Jesus.

Adeline was like night and day from that moment forward. Her daughter Lorna really noticed the change. She had finally become a beautiful, loving, Christian woman.

Cam had preached many times over the years, "What we sow, we must also reap." That truth was all too noticeable soon.

Approximately two years later, Adeline was on her death-bed suffering from cancer of the throat and a lifetime of over indulgence. One Saturday night Cam once again felt compelled to go visit with his sister, this time at the hospital.

The next morning Cam went to her side and prayed with her. He watched her struggle for life, gasping, gurgling, sucking air and not being able to get it, he could see the horror in her eyes as she was groping for something to hold on to. What a price to pay, he thought.

Adeline's second husband wished that she had quit smoking years ago. They had made plans to go and visit with his family that summer; all those plans were gone now. That is the way life is. If you put God out of your life, you will eventually pay the price.

Our bodies are temples of the Lord. God can't operate in a vessel that is contaminated with hate and sinful pleasures. Sins of the flesh will make you pay a staggering price in the long run. They will catch up with you and beat you down, physically and emotionally. Playing with death is a very dangerous game; smoking, drinking, drugging, it all takes its toll. Cam called upon his congregation to please learn by his example; he had been there and done that.

Adeline said that she wished she could live her life over again; she would have changed so much. She was under the impression that she could come back to the grace of God at any time she wanted. That is why she had chosen to take so long to give in to His will. The more one rebels against the Lord, the harder one becomes to reign in. The older you get, the harder it is to understand and accept the Lord into your life. Cam was quoted as saying, "Until the Holy Spirit draws you, you can't be drawn!"

After his visit with Adeline, Cam returned to his church. He had a sermon made out for that morning's service, but at the last moment he spoke from his heart about his sister and her lifestyle instead. By the end of his sermon, his lovely sister Adeline had passed away.

1985–1988

The following article is taken directly from our local paper, *The Nisqually Valley News.*

Thursday, March 6, 1986

Iversons to be honored

By Kristen Chamblee

An honorarium service will be held Sunday, March 9 in the Yelm Middle School gymnasium for Pastor Cam Iverson, 73, of Country Community Chapel and his wife, Gladys.

Service time is from 2:30 to 4:30 P.M. Community members have said about him, "He has been a good example for our community and has touched many hearts and lives." Everyone is invited to attend the occasion.

While Iverson said he is moved by the Sunday meeting, he candidly admitted, "I'd rather be heard and not seen." And so he does not want the focus to be on him but on God–who has done great things in Iverson's life and the life of his family members.

About God's presence in his life he said, "It's been just beautiful. If there's a chance to give God the glory, then I'm on the front line!"

Pastor Iverson's hope is to relay in his March 9 message an encouragement for families with sickness or trouble. "If God can do things for us, he can do it for everybody. Why not?" he said with enthusiasm.

For those who do not know Iverson's story, it is indeed miraculous. Iverson's parents, two brothers and two sisters came to Yelm in the fall of 1919. They lived in Canada and before that, Norway.

His father was a professional shoe cobbler and harness maker. He also began raising berries in Yelm.

Iverson can remember a Yelm of another era. There were dirt roads with horse and buggy carriages on the streets. A blacksmith shop, located where True Value Hardware store is now, was very active.

Pastor Iverson reached into his memory to recall dousing the town fire with buckets—the fire that destroyed the town of Yelm. At the time there were several stores, a drug store and a hotel that were lost, Iverson said.

His parents built the home that is located across from Messiah Stud stables on Yelm Highway and the five Iverson children attended Yelm schools until they graduated.

After graduation, Iverson did a stint with the Air Force for four and a half years that brought him to Gladys. Gladys was an English girl. They met in England, fell in love and married February 27.

The Iversons moved to Yelm on their first wedding anniversary. Iverson was employed at a veneer plant in Olympia for 22 years and worked for Western Farmers Co-op for 13 years.

During this time, Pastor Iverson did not live the

minister's life, or the 'straight and narrow path.' He watched his sister, Ruth, suffer from consumption of the ankle and bone and his brother, Hegge, from consumption of the lung, he explained.

Ruth was on crutches for seven years, had three surgeries, and was told the next time she would have to have the leg amputated.

Hegge was down to 97 pounds and not expected to live.

In the middle of the night, the Lord came to them. They dedicated their lives to His service and in turn, they were completely healed. The physician who attended his brother wrote, 'Not by man but by a higher power he was healed.'

Iverson's father watched the transformation in his children and gave his life over to Christ.

Meanwhile, Cam Iverson pondered these things.

On the outside, he was little changed. His wayward ways were still in his lifestyle. In his private moments, he secretly confessed to the Lord, "Here I am. If you will deliver me, clean me up, then I will be your servant as long as I live."

In June, 1965, when Iverson was 52 years old, he suffered a massive heart attack. In the ambulance, Iverson made a vow, "If you will spare my life, I will serve you for the rest of my days on earth."

He was basically crippled for two years following his near attack, so it was a very slow recovery—on the outside. On the inside, Cam Iverson was a changed man.

When the Lord healed his sister, she testified about her recovery on the radio, at colleges and other public places. She became known as "the miracle girl of Yelm." Later, Ruth became a missionary in Japan for 33 years.

Iverson's brother is currently the head of the Burden Bearers in Seattle, a Christian group that restores families, bringing them to relationships with Christ in their home and restoring unity.

Iverson explained, "I can talk to people who have problems because I was there." He added, "I have always asked the Lord to help me respect other's opinions." In the end, he said, he believes one's denomination has no bearing. It is what a person has done for Christ that counts.

Meanwhile, the little brown church in McKenna was in between pastors. Iverson was unable to work at a fulltime job because of his heart condition. The parishioners had heard of Cam Iverson's family and asked him to share his experiences. After hearing him speak, the little church asked him to be their pastor.

Iverson was astounded. He remembers praying, "Lord, I am not able. I am uneducated and untrained. I can't do it." And the vow he made in the ambulance came back to him as if a tape recorder was playing.

"I then prayed, forgive me, Lord. By your help, I will do the best I know how."

He added, "God is looking for availability, not ability. When we avail ourselves, He will give you the ability."

For a few years, he preached in McKenna. In the

mornings, he would build a fire in a wood stove to heat the Sunday school. "Many people attended and were converted," Iverson explained. "And the congregation was wonderful to me. They were great years," he said.

From McKenna, he preached in Yelm Middle School for four and a half years while Country Community Chapel was built on Morris Road.

Five acres were donated as the church site by parishioner, Ed Windsor. In November, 1979, the congregation moved into the basement of the building and in February, 1980, they moved into the church.

"We have been blessed with numerous people from various faiths joining our congregation. It has been rewarding, gratifying and consoling work. I would not have changed it for the world," Pastor Iverson said.

He explained how over half of the congregation came from families torn apart through strife or addiction. It was from this nucleus of believers the church was built. "You name the skill we needed, God provided a specific man or woman to do the job. It is just really exciting," he said.

For 13 years, he and assistant pastor, John Cook, served their congregation. Recently, Butch Halterman became the pastor and Iverson serves as the senior pastor. "There came a time when enough was enough," Iverson said simply.

The Iverson's have five children. All live in Yelm. They are Michael, 40, a store manager at Wolf's ShopRite for 23 years; Desmond, manager of Mega Foods in

Puyallup; Vernon, an employee at Yelm Telephone Company; Sharon Bellows, secretary in the Yelm School District administrative office and Darlene Rothwell, of Yelm Telephone Company. They have 12 grandchildren.

Iverson said quietly, "I have lived what I confess and have tried to be the father they can respect. It has worked out and I am grateful." He said all his children have been wholehearted backers of his ministry.

As far as retiring his work for the Lord, Iverson said, "I am going to occupy myself with His work until I leave this world."

"The greatest effective ministry today is love. It is not preaching, it is showing that you care. Love thrives on love and it dies for the lack of it. That goes for everything—in the home, family relationships—everything." Iverson concluded.

At Cam's honorarium in 1986, when introducing him to the folks gathered there, Gladys quoted a line she had read in The Olympian paper that week. "Look at me with your heart, your eyes might not see so good." Cam was a professional at just that.

Pastor Cam's Departure

Controversy caused Pastor Cam to leave the Country Community Chapel in April of 1986. It is said that the newer younger congregants enjoyed the easygoing sermons of the newer, younger, well-educated pastor. They complained about Cam's repetition of messages. The older congregants favored Cam and his "fire and brimstone" style, pounding in the messages until they were loud and clear.

Cam was virtually silent during the entire transition period when it seemed to him as though he was on his way out of his own church. I can only imagine what must have been going through his mind at that time. Some of his congregation had branded him as a no-fighter, a man without a backbone. He claimed to be a peacemaker, not a fighter. He chose his silent stance intentionally.

Cam very much believed in practicing what he preached, and wouldn't say a bad word about the new pastor or anyone for that matter. He had very strong feelings that their church was not healthy in spirit. Agree or not, their church was sick in fellowship. What used to be a full house was no longer, and what used to be loving friendships were no longer. Congregants had picked sides and many members had left altogether. The transition blinded many people.

Some said that the new Pastor and Cam were facing off in a power struggle. Cam didn't see it that way at all, at least not on his part. He had never once desired any authority, or excessive authority for that matter, over anyone. He never demanded to have his own way "or else," he didn't believe in that kind of mindset. Cam had always felt small, insignificant, and very inadequate in the eyes of God and the eyes of his peers. Oftentimes he would pray, "Dear God, I need your help," just to make it through a day. He realized that he was "nothing" in the eyes of God, just a mere man professing his faith to the common people.

The effect of the transition on the personal relationships Cam had with his flock was absolutely devastating. Many of his closest lifelong friends were miles apart emotionally and spiritually. There was a "cold dampness" where there used to be warmth and blessing.

Cam had said that the new Pastor was a very capable and well-educated pastor, but that their ministries were very different. The new Pastor was very "new age" with his ministry. Cam's ministry checked everything from lifestyle, attitude, and speech, to everyday living. He wished his congregation could go back to their spiritual "diapers" and be "broken" before God, and advised them not to let *anything* or *anyone* rob them of their tenderness with God.

Choosing sides and showing favoritism was wrong and sinful. Cam was deeply wounded and hurt that some of his sheep had gone to other churches and were now scattered across the town. They had lost tremendous strength and it was extremely discouraging. He felt as though these people were his personal flock and he didn't want to simply let them walk away. He said that if he could have, he would have guided them back one by one individually.

Cam had a great understanding of why people do things because he took the time to sit down to talk with them and listen to them. Time was no boundary for him. He made it a point to make sure that he knew his congregation inside and out. He knew in his heart why people were leaving Country Community Chapel and it bothered him down to the root of his very soul.

"I am as dumb as they make them, but I am RICH in GOD!" he professed to his church. Cam thanked God for what little he knew, and what little he had. "I will be a pastor until the day I die! No one can take that away from me. God gave it to me. God chose me." He said he could play the role of an elder in the church, but he only wanted to be their pastor. He knew in his heart what was coming next. The pain and agony was growing hourly.

In one of his last talks with his congregation he warned them that a curse would befall their holy temple. Was it prophecy or simply intuition?

The new Pastor and the congregants had planned an auction for the following Sunday on church grounds. That was against the very Testament that Cam had spent the past 20 years preaching. There was to be absolutely no buying or selling on a

Sunday, especially not in the Lord's house of prayer! The church was not a merchandise house and Cam felt it was totally wrong. He felt very strongly about this issue, and begged them not to go forward with their plans.

There was also a dance being planned for that weekend which he felt would only lead to more sin and was a very dangerous road for them to follow. At the time, news stories were filled with teenager's lack of self-control and severe lack of morals. Cam then asked his congregation, "If we can't function and work together here as a church, how can we do it in heaven?" It was a thought for everyone to ponder.

I just got done reading a letter from a Canadian about the current situation our country and the world as a whole is faced with. She suggested going back to the good ole' days when humanity had some sort of morality and integrity and most people followed the rules and laws as they were written. Maybe there was some good advice in Cam's wholesome preaching . . .

What follows is a letter of resignation from Cam and Gladys when they had finally had enough of the constant struggle.

April 27, 1986

Country Community Chapel
13042 Morris Road S.E.
Yelm, Washington 98597

Dear Country Community Chapel Congregation:

Just over 18 years ago, we were led by the Lord to take over the pastorate at McKenna Community Church. This started as an exciting ministry with God's blessings and approval. Souls were saved continually in the 7-½ years we were there.

The next 4-½ years we worshipped with enthusiasm at the Yelm Middle School Classatorium and worked together to build the Country Community Chapel. We have been here for approximately 6 years. This temple has been our life. We have done the best we knew how and feel our hearts are pure before God.

Last Friday night around 9:45, we had a visit from six (6) of the Chapel's men with a petition signed by the followers of Pastor (name removed for privacy) asking Pastor Cam and Gladys for their resignation. At first, after a fast review, we declined because the election was illegal, since it was not announced for 2 weeks in advance for the whole body to participate, according to the bylaws of the Chapel.

However, after much thought and asking the Lord for direction to do what was pleasing to Him, we both felt the Holy Spirit would have us leave now and not stay where we are no longer wanted. We have loved and cared for this flock and leave with a hurting and broken heart. God will open up new doors of ministry for us as we continue to do His will.

Goodbye to you all! Cam's voice has been silenced.

Pastor Cam Iverson
Gladys Iverson

Cam never would talk about what happened. Neither would Gladys. Suffice it to say, God allowed it for a reason.

He and Gladys attended the Yelm Prairie Christian Center after their departure from the Country Community Chapel in 1986. Cam continued to lead his flock spiritually to the best of his ability, through prayer and small services in private homes, without the aid of a pulpit to stand behind.

Gladys & Cam's 40th Anniversary

A Pastor for the People

It does not matter what denomination you are. What you are doing for Jesus is what counts. Cam felt very strongly about this concept. Your relationship with Jesus and those around you tells far more about you than how often you have Father Flanagan over for Sunday supper does.

How many times do we hear about corruption within the Catholic Church, or the Protestant Church, or the Mormon Church for that matter? There is a war of religions going on, it is a huge power struggle to be the "right" one. The funny thing about that concept is that traditionally there is only One God, only One Jesus, only One Holy Ghost. Look around you and open up your eyes. We can't even count how many churches are out there, how many denominations, how many belief systems, and how many variations of the same theme there are. When are we going to get back to the basics of a simple faith?

Pastor Cam was loved so dearly because it didn't matter to

him which church you went to and the people here knew that. He loved the title of Pastor, or just plain Brother Cam, because it made him feel good about himself and his ability to share with his community. He felt like he was giving something back. If you needed ministering, he was there at your side. If you needed faith, he had an abundance of it to share.

Oftentimes, he was called upon by other "faiths" to minister to "their" people. He was always more than happy to oblige. His flock was wherever he was needed at the time, whether it was in the church, a parking lot, or at a shopping mall. Many people to this day still remember, and appreciated his willingness to be so open and loving to people of all walks of life. His ability to relate to the "simple" man was incredibly powerful.

Gladys especially loved Cam's genuine devotion to the Lord. He was so friendly with everyone he met and had such boldness about him. If a person had a certain look on their face while walking through the grocery store, Cam's arm would soon be around their shoulder and they would soon be joining him in prayer. Cam would witness his faith to anyone, anywhere, at any time. He had no boundaries, no blocks, nothing standing in his way. He emanated the spirit of a true Christian.

September 1987

LAURA M. PORRAS

A Call to The People

1987 was a hard year for Cam. He had open-heart surgery and was recovering nicely. The photo above was taken in September of 1987 just before Cam and Gladys boarded a plane to Hawaii. His children came together with the funds to have a chauffer-driven limo take them from their home in Yelm to the airport in Seattle. Sharon and Darlene, their two daughters, went along for the ride.

Cam had always wanted to go to Hawaii because he loved the sunshine. He and Gladys would soon be off on their dream vacation for two weeks in a sunny paradise. Sadly, three days after arriving at their destination, Cam and Gladys had to return home.

Every time Cam went out to the beach and got sun, his legs would ache so bad from the exposure to the very sun he loved, that he had go back inside. Unbeknownst to him, this was a classic symptom of the bone cancer that was yet to be diagnosed. Also while there, he developed a major cough. Gladys thought he might develop pneumonia so they decided it was best to simply return home.

In June of 1988 Campbell Iverson was finally diagnosed with the bone cancer. Gladys' nerves were shot by this time; she was later prescribed sedatives to help calm her down because so much was going on and it seemed as though there was no calm in sight. Cam's brother Bob had heard about an alternative treatment program in Mexico involving laetrile, which reportedly killed cancers cells in the patient's blood stream.

Laetrile is another name for the chemical amygdalin, which is found in the pits of many fruits and is also found in many plants. Cyanide was thought to be its main anticancer component. Laetrile was first used as a cancer treatment in Russia in 1845 and then again in the United States in the 1920's.

Laetrile has not been approved for use in the US for various disputed reasons. Many positive case studies have been reported and documented throughout recent history. Still, the United States has chosen to ban it.

Genesis 1:29 "And God said, Behold I have given you every herb bearing seed, which is upon the face of all the earth, and every tree, in the which is the fruit of a tree yielding seed; to you it shall be for meat." The Bible tells us in plain language that everything we need to survive and be healthy is readily available right here on earth.

Vitamin B-17, another name for Laetrile, is found in most fruit seeds. Apples, peaches, cherries, grapes, apricots, bitter almonds, millet, lima beans and many grasses such as wheat grass, all have B-17 in them.

Apricot seeds are said to have the highest content of B-17 on earth. They used to be readily available on most store shelves until the FDA did raids on grocers all over the country and removed them. The hard pit in the middle of the apricot or peach was never supposed to be thrown away; the shell is actually a strong armor protecting the seed that carries the nutrient we all needed.

This is one of the main courses of food in completely cancer free cultures such as the Navajo Indians, the Hunzakuts, the Abkhazians, the Eskimos, and many more.

As a preventative, Dr. Ernst Krebs, the scientist who discovered B-17, said that seven or more apricot seeds per day would make it impossible to develop cancer in one's lifetime. One or two of the 100 mg B-17 tablets would be an acceptable supplemental daily dosage. Stores no longer sell "raw" apricot seeds because of those raids I mentioned earlier. The FDA made stocking vitamin B-17 and apricot seeds somewhat of a Federal Crime.

In March of 1984 the government brought in The Medicines Order 1984 (Cyanogenetic Substances). This meant "preparations which are presented for sale or supply under the name of, or as containing, amygdalin, laetrile or vitamin B-17 or contain more than 0.1 percent by weight of the 'cyanide-producing substances' were to be under the control of the 1968 Medicines Act". Therefore, Laetrile is now out of easy reach to any and all cancer patients being treated in the United States who would prefer exercising his or her own freedom of choice.

1 Corinthians 1:27 says, "But God hath chosen the foolish things of the world to confound the wise; and God hath chosen the weak things of the world to confound the things which are mighty." Why does this concept sound so familiar? See the comments above for an answer.

The book "World Without Cancer" by Mr. Edward Griffin holds a lot of information on actual case studies that were covered up. It also tells of the great scientists who were arrested when they began informing others about the truth of the curing powers of vitamin B-17.

"If the American Medical Association, the FDA and the American Cancer Society had tried to ban Laetrile, it must be of considerable value in treating cancer." (Rattigan)

As a result of not having the FDA approval, the various court cases against doctors, the over abundance of federal funding for drug manufacturing companies, and the "alleged" cover-ups by the government, the use of laetrile as a cancer therapy is not approved in the United States. It continues to be manufactured and administered as an anticancer treatment primarily in Mexico.

"If the people let the government decide what foods they eat and what medicines they take, their bodies will soon be in as sorry a state as the souls who live under tyranny." - Thomas Jefferson

Following is a brief description of the Harold Manner Clinic that used to be in Tijuana, Mexico. I couldn't find any current information on the clinic, so I am under the impression that it is no longer in operation.

Harold Manner Clinic, Tijuana, Mexico

Heraclio Bernal #1, Fracc. Soler, C.P. 22100, Tijuana
011 (526) 630–5869 / 011 (526) 630–5870
U.S.: Harold Manner Memorial Hospital - PMB 63
P.O. Box 439056, San Diego, CA 92143–9056
PO Box 434290, San Ysidro, CA 92143–4290
1 (800) 433–4962/1 (800) 248–8431

"Oh yes, it does work, and I have documented case studies of work done with both laboratory animals and human beings which prove that nutrition therapy using Laetrile can cure, contain, and prevent cancer."- Harold W. Manner, Ph.D

Doctor Manner took over the Cydel Hospital in Tijuana and renamed it the Manner Clinic, which as far as I could ascertain, continued to offer the "Manner cocktail" into the 90's despite Dr. Manner's death in October of 1988. The clinic was temporarily shut down but they reopened it after reorganization. The Hospital was located just a few miles south of San Diego on the outskirts of Tijuana, and they treated cancer for well over two decades.

A typical course of treatment usually lasted about three weeks, and could have been extended to 90 days depending on the individual patient's situation. This particular treatment reportedly caused a 90 percent complete cure of cancer in rats. After an evaluation by the hospital staff, a course of therapy was customized and prescribed. This therapy usually included detoxification, nutritional supplementation, diet, and rest. Most of their patients were considered "terminal."

Patients received a daily Intra-venous drip of Laetrile, vitamins, trace minerals, DMSO (technically called dimethyl sufoxide, which is a by-product of the wood industry and has been used as a commercial solvent since 1953. DMSO penetrates the skin quickly and deeply without damaging it and eases pain) and proteolytic enzymes, which have been known to break up biological products.

Proteolytic enzymes are used for assistance in the repairing and the healing of the body, and in clinical trials during the 1950's they were shown to aid in maintaining a healthy respiratory system. The specific combinations and potencies of each of these products depended upon the doctor's evaluation of the individual needs of each patient.

If a patient's immune system has been weakened from things like poor nutrition, environmental pollutants, or debilitating stress, the cancer cells are left virtually uninhibited and will multiply rapidly. This is what is commonly viewed as the "growth" of cancer. The objective of all the therapies that I came across in my research was to essentially revitalize the body's immune system, thereby restoring it to a fully functional condition.

It is said that we can remain healthy and virtually disease free if we supply the cells of our bodies with the proper amounts of oxygen, nutrients, enzymes, minerals, amino acids and other essential elements from both our diet and additional nutritional supplements. Equally important is the ability of our bodies to eliminate the waste products of cellular metabolism through bowel movements, efficient breathing, normal excretion, etc.

Treatments must be provided which will help the body detoxify itself by eliminating harmful pollutants.

The Manner Clinic had been called the "world leader in disease prevention" and promised treatment based on "the latest scientific and medical information." Employees met the patients at the San Diego airport and took them in a white van across the border into Mexico. Patients didn't need passports because they weren't going any further south than Tijuana, but they were asked to bring their medical records. Many clinics within a reasonable distance from the California Mexico border still operate this way. There has been a rush South to take care of our bodies and our spirits in recent years.

The decision was made that Cam would try this form of treatment and that his daughter Sharon would accompany him on the trip, as she was the only family member available at the time, even though she had just moved to Vermont the month before with her family. The cost of the program was in excess of $10,000.

Cam and Gladys went down to their local bank and applied for a personal loan. A friend of the family, Velma Curry, who worked for the local telephone company, took the dilemma into her own hands. She took it upon herself to go down to the local newspaper and take out an ad asking the community for help.

Fund Established to Offset Medical Costs

Originally printed in the **Nisqually Valley News**

As a pastor, Cam Iverson has been a part of weddings and baptisms, of funerals and births. In times of joy and in times of sadness, Pastor Cam has been there to share the tears. For some who were in the hospital, his visit and words of encouragement gave the sense that someone cared.

In times of crisis, any in the community could call on

Cam for assistance. It mattered little to Cam whether the person in need was a member of his congregation. What mattered was that there was a need and he could fill it.

Cam Iverson now faces a crisis of his own. In his time of need, it seems appropriate that the community he has helped so many times should somehow repay him. In Cam's battle against bone cancer, the Iverson family has been faced with many medical expenses.

To help the family with these costs, a fund has been established at Prairie Security Bank to receive donations. Those wishing to contribute can receive more information at the bank.

To Gladys' amazement, the people gave back to Cam in abundance. The collection taken up for Cam's care covered nearly all of the $10,000. In July of 1988, Cam and his daughter Sharon made the southward trek to Mexico for treatment.

Cam during treatment in Mexico

While in Tijuana, Cam made amazing progress. He arrived in a wheelchair, unable to walk. The doctors gave him a complete physical and found twenty-one ailments, from high blood pressure to arthritis attacking his body.

Not one for sitting around and waiting to get better, Cam took to his Bible and became a Chaplain after about one week in treatment. With Sharon at his side, he began visiting and ministering to other patients in the hospital. Cam actually had people knocking on his door asking him to pray for them! It was a mission field.

One of his doctors had a patient who was comatose and completely unresponsive. Cam was asked to pray for this man, as there was nothing else that anyone could do; politely and humbly he obliged him. Amazingly, shortly after praying for him, the comatose man awoke! The power of prayer is a wonderful thing.

The medical facility psychologist made it a point to visit with all of the patients to make sure that they were in a healthy state of mind. The key to success of any treatment program, whether it is physical or mental, is a positive attitude.

Cam was so much further along than most with a positive outlook that they deemed his visit with the Psychologist unnecessary. All those around him were taken in by his spirit and faith. The psychologist even told him that he could use his help around there! He wanted to work with Cam as a team to bring about healing for the other patients.

Through treatment with Laetrile and good old-fashioned faith and prayer, by the time he left three weeks after arriving, all but two of his ailments had completely gone away and he was able to move around without the aid of his wheelchair. At his return, Cam was considered to be doing well.

August 1988

Note of thanks

A few weeks ago a caring friend placed an article in this newspaper concerning medical expenses for Cam Iverson as he was taking treatments in Mexico for the diagnosed bone cancer.

A fund was set up at our new Prairie Security Bank.

The response was overwhelming. We want to express our special thanks publicly, later we will write to you all individually.

Many could not help financially, but gave prayer support, letters, cards and flowers–thanks to you all.

Not only did all the help supply the monetary need, but Cam and daughter, Sharon (who went with him) were able to minister and pray for lots of hurting people. You too shared in that as you reached out to us.

Cam is progressing each day, is on a 90-day treatment program and plans shortly, God willing, to be again visiting and sharing in his parish of Yelm!

Thanks
Pastor Cam and Gladys Iverson and family

*Originally printed in the **Nisqually Valley News***

Cam's daughter Sharon believes that the Mexico treatments probably added two months of prime time of good health to her Dad's life. Unfortunately, as anyone of us would, Cam got tired of the daily ritual of consuming one medication after the other every hour on the hour only to extend his life. The cost of the medications was becoming a tremendous financial burden. He decided that if God wanted him to come home, who was he to prolong that effort? He stopped taking all of his medications and made the slow journey downhill physically and emotionally.

While he was ill at the VA hospital in Seattle, Cam would oftentimes pray with his nurses and other patients. This took everyone by surprise, but was not totally unexpected. To the very end, the word of God was leading him home.

It didn't take much longer for the stresses of a lifetime of adversity and challenge to take him over.

Sharon received a phone call, from her sister Darlene, at her home back East in Vermont the night before her father died. He had fallen into a coma and she needed to come home. She was told that her Father had gone to the Doctor for a check up, as he wasn't feeling well. X-rays were taken because Cam's lungs were filling with water. During this process he had to hold his arms above his head for long periods of time. Every movement hurt him at that point. After the x-rays were taken, a male nurse literally threw Cam very roughly back in his bed. "You hurt me!" he cried out. Cam was given extensive amounts of morphine to control the pain.

Darlene complained to the doctor that she felt her Dad was being overmedicated. His reply back to her was, "Would you rather have your Dad in constant pain?" Sharon believes that the overmedication lead to the coma. Members of the family kept telling Cam to hold on until his beloved Sharon could get there. She spent the entire following day in the air trying to get home, worried sick the whole flight, praying that she would make it in time for her final goodbye.

The entire afternoon, family and friends were gathered around his bedside singing songs of praise to him before his transition in to Heaven. Sharon waited until everyone else had said his or her final goodbyes to him. She and her sister-in-law Debbie were the last ones by his side. At that time she took her father's hand. She said to him, "Dad, you lived a good life, you can go home now, we will take care of Mom," thereby releasing him from his earthly duties. Five minutes later, to the peaceful tune of "The Hem of His Garment" playing on a tape player, he went to heaven.

The Lord's Shepherd Rests in Peace

On November 30, 1988, twelve days before he was to celebrate his 75th birthday, at 2:21 A.M., God put in His last call to a very loyal shepherd.

Campbell Iverson, at 74 years of age, took his final breath without any pomp or circumstance. He had been in steadily declining health at the Black Hills Community Hospital in Olympia, Washington.

The death certificate lists the immediate cause of his death as intracranial hemorrhage, that is the pathological accumulation of blood within the cranial vault due to thrombocytopenia, which is a disorder in which the number of platelets, a type of blood cell, is abnormally low, sometimes associated with abnormal bleeding and multiple myeloma, which is a cancer of the bone marrow for which there is currently no known cure.

His family believes to this day that he died prematurely of a broken heart due to the circumstances surrounding his departure from Country Community Chapel.

The day after his death, Sharon called Judy Dutra and asked if she and her husband Frank would have a special number for the service. Judy sang and Frank played the saxophone. Judy asked what they wanted her to play. Sharon suggested that Judy pick something. Judy said how about "The Hem of His Garment"; funny as how that was his passing music. Sharon said that would be a perfect song.

Funeral services were held in the Yelm Middle School Commons, a place he knew very well, and had preached from often, on December 4, 1988 at 2:00 PM. More than anything, the family wanted this not to be a day of mourning, but instead to be a joyful time in celebration of a life well lived. It was a very musical and upbeat service. The room was filled with approximately 600 seats and not very many of them were empty.

Cam's brother Bob gave an amazing eulogy. There was not a dry eye in the house. He told a story of when Cam and Hegge stole alfalfa from a neighbor's barn as a prank. They were dumbstruck as to how that neighbor found out they had been the ones that had taken it. The boys had forgotten all about the snow outside that was covering the ground. As they had walked from the barn to their house, a little trail of alfalfa was marking their route. All that the neighbor had to do was follow the green path to find the boys. Everyone in the Commons was laughing heartily at that!

Bob also mentioned a motto that Cam had always lived by. It was the theory of the four P's: Possibilities, People, Performance, and Potential. Cam believed in everyone. He believed in what could happen, what people could do and what we could become.

Gladys never knew where the key to the prayer room had been kept. She wasn't ever allowed in there to clean. It was a most sacred place. On the door outside was posted a sign that said "Take off your shoes, this is holy ground." She found out later from her daughter Sharon that the key was kept in the chicken house!

Thank you for Cam Iverson!

Cam's Death Certificate

Cam's Casket

I have decided to include some of the condolences and personal notes that were sent to the family upon Cam's death. You can judge for yourself how many lives one man touched through the power of God.

Who was Campbell Iverson asks a loving grandson

*Originally printed in the **Nisqually Valley News***

To all of you who didn't know "Cam" and what he stood for, he was a true man of God, and he was my Grandpa. There isn't many like him around any more. Not many people today can preach with a meaning like my Grandpa did when he was alive.

He was the type of person who would go help pray for those who were sick, alcoholics, or the cast outs that no one else wanted. That's what made him the man that he was here on earth, and that's what he's being rewarded for in heaven. It says in the Bible that only what we do on earth with Christ will last.

My Grandpa used to be an alcoholic over 50 years ago, one you didn't want to be around. One day, though, he decided to give his life to the Lord because of the prayers of his mother. He was a very loving and caring man to everyone he came in contact with, whether they were great or small.

While he was a pastor the last 20 years, he had several heart attacks and close calls with death. Do you think that would stop him from doing the Lord's work? No way, not my Grandpa! He would still get out of bed and preach sermons and help people out, no matter how much pain he was in. Even before he passed away, he prayed for a nurse the day before.

Grandpa helped build a million-dollar church and never once begged for money. God supplied every need, over and above. He loved people. Grandpa was very hurt when he was no longer wanted as pastor of that church, but he never said one bad word against any of them. His heart was broken, and I believe he died a premature death because of it. If only they were kinder, he might be alive today.

I love my Grandpa dearly, and he meant everything in the world to me. I'm going to try to follow in the footsteps of him. He was a true example of what a man of God should be. I'll see him soon in heaven.

Jon Bellows, Jr., first grandson

Jon Sr., Jody, Jon Jr., Sharon, & Cam

From his funeral

Only one life 'twill soon be past; only what we do for Christ will last.

"Precious in the sight of the Lord is the death of his saints." (Psalms 116:15)

THERE IS A REASON

There's a reason for everything;
A reason to live, and a reason to die.
Most of the time we don't know why
God chooses to allow one of His children to die.
And if you should feel hurt or pain,
Just remember that "Our God Reigns."
It says in the Bible that our Lord will come again one day;
And when that day comes, all of His children will go.
But for some people, sooner than you and I know.
What happened to my Grandpa is really sad.
Yet, I know my Jesus must need him so bad.

So now that he's gone to his original home,
A place where forever with Jesus he'll roam.
So if for my Grandpa you should shed a tear,
Remember, for him in death was no fear.
For on this earth my Grandpa's work is all done,
And he now hears the words, "Welcome Home, My Son."

By Jody Bellows (Grandson)

Opening Prayer–Pastor Robert Iverson

"Rivers of Babylon"–Grandchildren
By the rivers of Babylon where we sat down,
Yeah, we wept when we remembered Zion.
Carry us away in captivity required from us a song;
Now, how shall we sing the Lord's song in a strange land.
Let the words of our mouths and the
meditation of our hearts be acceptable
in thy sight here tonight.

Eulogy–Pastor Dan Schaefer

"This is Your Crowning Day"–Darlene Rothwell

Poem–Michael Iverson

"The Hem of His Garment"–Frank & Judy Dutra

"What a Day That Will Be"–Darlene Rothwell & Debbie
Iverson

Sermon–Pastor Robert Iverson

"I Want to Stroll Over Heaven"–Debbie Iverson

A PROMISE TO GOD

Closing Prayer–Pastor Kevin Sample

Burial followed at the Yelm Cemetery. There were refreshments in the banquet room of the Nisqually Valley Restaurant afterwards. Everyone was given a cordial invitation.

BLESS YOU!
(One of Pastor Cam's favorite sayings)

" . . . Well done, good and faithful servant . . ."
Mattew 25:23
(The passage above is printed on Cam's tombstone.)

Heaven's Blessedness
By Barbara Ann Oudean

I'll walk the golden streets one day
And hear my heavenly Father say

Well done! Thou good and faithful son
The harvest's in, Your work is done

You've labored long down through the years
You've prayed and shed those tears

Now is time for you to rest
To share in heaven's Blessedness

Dedicated to:
Pastor Cam Iverson
Yelm Country Community Chapel

Originally printed in the *Nisqually Valley News*

LAURA M. PORRAS

From a letter to the Editor of the *Nisqually Valley News:*

A Man of God
by A. Yeager

A face familiar to us all,
Like a dear image in a locket.
To the children, a Christian Pied Piper,
With candy in his pocket.

Thinking himself an average man,
Not worthy of any award,
He would shrink from special recognition,

Draw back from human reward.
Yet we would have him know our thanks,

For those years of sacrifice;
Pastoring a church, visiting the sick,
Hours of prayer for us, that had a price.

Called to countless duties, he answered -

Physically suffering, but sustained.
Wherever needed, there he'd be,

Constantly filling . . . nearly drained.

The world smiles on the
Arrogant,

Marching through life full of
Pride,

A PROMISE TO GOD

While our friend has a humble heart,
That has been wounded, tested and tried.

But that unassuming manner
Is what draws us like bees to honey;
To a comfortable man,
Who cares nothing for power or money.

Is there any higher compliment,
Any term, however broad,
That speaks of honor due more fully,
Than "He's a man of God?"

We do not lift you higher than the rest,
To a seat you would not take.
We just say, "Love has lived through you;"
May we be imitators for all our sakes.

And so we honor you, Pastor,
For the loving deed you've done:

And describe you thus, "A man of God,"
Yelm's own Cam Iverson

December 1, 1988

My dear Gladys,

I feel your heart, your tears, your hurt! He is in heaven! How difficult it is to let go. How wonderful it is to know we will be reunited with our loved ones. You must be so proud of your husband. The love he had for you and his children. The love he gave to so many. His faith in God he ministered to hundreds and thousands. He set the example of belief to his children, grand-children and friends. He built a foundation of love, trust, and faith in God on a rock. How blessed you will be to have the fruit of his teaching in each of your children and their children. This will give you love and strength. Cam will keep his arms around you until you meet in heaven. He's preparing a place for you in heaven as he loved you and took care of you on earth. He's your guardian angel.

I love you,
Peggy (Wolf)

A PROMISE TO GOD

"He Went Home for Christmas"
by Rosemary Lambert
Elma, Washington

Original publication date and place unknown

For the memory of Cam Iverson, a devoted saint of the
Lord, who was loved and appreciated by many.

He went home for Christmas,
But left it all behind;
The tinsel, lights, and glitter gay,
And gifts of every king.
He went home for Christmas,
This long awaited day,
Yet those of us who said goodbye
So wished that he could stay.
He went home for Christmas,
While bells of heaven rang.
The golden gate swing wide for him,
And hosts of Angels sang.
He went home for Christmas,
His humble praise to bring;
Yes . . . he went home at
Christmas time,
For the birthday of his King.

Dear Gladys,

If my human love for you was perfect, I'd set you free from hurting today. All the things you've prayed for would have come to be. There wouldn't be this awful separation from the mate you chose all those years ago. And I'd give you a body strong and new, forever protected from any attack. Sadness would never touch your heart, and joy is all you'd know. I'd see you released from disappointment and mourning, not even remembering what those words mean.

But as it is—I can only be with you in a VERY small way—with what you're going through. We must all wait for the Lord to bring us to His perfection. He is the only One who can bring about the things I've mentioned, and how totally without hope we would be without Him.

I love you Gladys Dear, and will take this occasion to say, I deeply appreciate the role you've lived as a pastor's wife. All of the hard work behind the scenes, and on the front lines. All of the visits, calls, gifts, cooking and prayers. All of the sleepless nights.

You've been an example and an inspiration to so many of us. Your advice to me has always been full of wisdom. I need you!

Although you're tired, and suffering more than I can know- please don't give up. There are scores of us women who truly need what you can give. Even a few words over the telephone from you, have changed my attitude for the better!

Our Pastor Cam was blessed to have you as his wife, and he knew it well.

Your sister in the Lord,
Audrey (Yeager)

May God Be With You

Dear Gladys and family,

How our hearts go out to you today! Patsy just called to tell us of Cam's graduation. What a glorious homecoming for him!

There are not enough words to express the love we feel for all of you, for our thankfulness for the love, the giving, the sharing, the serving, the blessing your family has been and is -- always *giving, giving, giving,* of your whole selves for Christ. Even today, right in the midst of your own sorrow, Mike, you asked Patsy about Milt Butler and expressed Cam's deep concern for his salvation. How typical!

Gladys, most of all, you are in my heart. What a devoted wife and mother! What an example for every woman! Blessed art thou, Gladys! May you now more than ever before feel God's love surrounding you and His peace filling your heart. How grateful we are for all the blessed promises!

Our family is but one among the *many* extending our tribute to Cam for his faithful ministry to so many over the years. We can think of no one more deserving to hear our blessed Lord say, "Well done, good and faithful servant." We'll all miss him!

Love and blessings,
Doyal and Julie Gallagher

Sharing Your Loss

"Cam" touched the hearts of *so many people* . . . and so many loved him, and will miss him. I am sure Heaven is pleased to have him there but Earth is a poorer place.
Love to all of you.
Bless you all.

Betty and Hugh Long

Whatsoever Things Are True

Dear Cam,

Thank you so much for all the kind things you have done
for my family throughout the years.

Thanks so much for the beautiful Christian witness you
have been in our community.

All of us love you deeply and our thoughts and prayers are
with you daily.

From one raspberry grower to another–with love,

Your sister,
Cindy Cecil

God's Love Is Near You

Dear Gladys,

We have always had so much respect for Pastor Cam. He holds a special place in our hearts . . . God used him to bring us (and many others) to salvation. We know that his rewards in heaven are *very* great.

We love you and your family and wish you the best

Love,
Jack and Sally Lizee and Girls

Jack went on to become a Pastor here in Yelm. He was one of two of Cam's congregants to carry on in the service of the Lord.

May God's Love Comfort You

To Aunt Gladys and Family,

Please accept my sincere condolences on the passing of Uncle Cam. He left a legacy of faith and humility for us to follow.

With love,
Randal (Frivold)

What God Hath Promised

Just want you to know that Cam had a tremendous influence on me as a teenager. He was so faithful each Sunday to minister to our high school class!

In Christ,
Laverne (Beggs) Gibbs

A PROMISE TO GOD

Treasured Memories of a Loved One

Treasured memories of a beloved husband, father,
and grandfather, Campbell Iverson, who the
Lord called home on November 30, 1988.

We lost the one with a heart of gold;
How much we miss him can never be told.
He shared our troubles and helped us along;
If we walk in his footsteps, we will never go wrong.
In our hearts he will always stay,
Loved and remembered everyday.

His wife Gladys and
children, Michael, Sharon,
Desmond, Vernon, Darlene
and their families
11–30–90

Originally printed in the *Nisqually Valley News*

Note of Thanks

Here we are again, expressing our heartfelt thanks to our wonderful friends for all the love and support during Cam's illness and passing to glory.

The flowers, cards, telephone calls and memorial gifts were all deeply appreciated.

Also thanks to the ladies of the Yelm Prairie Assembly of God for all the delicious meals brought to the house and the efficient catering for our family and friends following the funeral.

This is indeed a caring community, we are blessed.

Also thanks to the Yelm police for their escort and the military for their gun salute and taps at the graveside.

We appreciate all of you that came out to support us last Sunday as we said farewell to a loving husband, father, grandfather and friend. Bless you all.

Gladys Iverson
Michael Iverson and family
Sharon Bellows and family
Desmond Iverson and family
Vernon Iverson and family
Darlene Rothwell and family

Originally printed in the *Nisqually Valley News*

Memorial for a Family Member

To the Editor:
Enclosed are a few treasured memories of a dear husband,
father, and grandfather, Cam Iverson, who passed away on
November 30, 1988.

> Many years you have lived,
> but by the love you gave,
> and the things you did.
> Your pleasures were simple,
> your needs were few.
> When your family was happy,
> so were you.
> Though no longer
> in our lives to share,
> in our thoughts you will
> always be there.
> You taught us many things in
> life that we would have to do,
> but you never taught us how
> to hide the hurt of losing you!

Thank you,
wife, Gladys and his children, Michael, Sharon,
Desmond, Vernon, Darlene and their families

11–89
Originally printed in the *Nisqually Valley News*

LAURA M. PORRAS

In memory of Pastor Iverson

To the Editor:
With fondest memories of our loved one, Pastor Campbell
Iverson, who was called to his heavenly home on November 30,
1988.

One or the other must leave,
One or the other must stay.
One or the other must grieve,
that is forever the way.
That is the vow that was sworn,
faithful 'til death do us part.
Braving what had to be borne,
hiding the ache in the heart.
One, howsoever adored,
first must be summoned away
That is the will of the Lord
one or the other must stay.
"Sunset in one land is sunrise
in another."

From the wife and family
he left behind

11–25–93
Originally printed in the *Nisqually Valley News*

A LOVING MEMORY 11–92

Family members remember Campbell Iverson

In loving memory of a dear husband, father, grandfather and community pastor who was called to his heavenly home on November 30, 1988.

Along the road of yesterday,
that takes us back to you,
Our memory of us all together
and the happy times we knew.
In our thoughts forever you will stay,
In each and every passing day,
Time may pass and fade away
but silent thoughts and memories stay.

The family of Campbell Iverson

Originally printed in the *Nisqually Valley News*

Campbell Iverson is Remembered fondly

In loving memory of a very special husband, dad and grandpa, Campbell Iverson, who was called home to be with his Lord on November 30, 1988:

Precious forever our
memories of you,
So they will remain our
whole life through.
Though absent you are
always near,
Still loved, still missed and so
very dear.
Though heaven and earth
divide us,
And the distance seems a lot,
There is a flower that blooms
between us,
the sweet forget-me-not.

His wife, children and their families

11–28–91
Originally printed in the *Nisqually Valley News*

A PROMISE TO GOD

This message came all the way from England and was originally printed in one of their papers, publication date and source unknown.

JOHNSON
Our dear parents
Blanche Victoria,
Sydney Harry
Also brother-in-law
Campbell Iverson (U.S.A.)
With every day that passes
We seem to find a way
To wander back and
meet you
On the road to yesterday.
Joy, Malcolm, Joyce,
Walter, Irene, George
and Gladys (U.S.A.)

To my dear Sharon,

God truly heard your prayers. I have been thinking about you and your family with a fielded heart. Your father is in heaven, united with our Father. The promise your father spoke to so many, he has given to his wife, his children and grandchildren and family his awareness of God. He has touched hundreds. How proud you must be to have the foundation of your life given to you by blood and spirit. You have been a devoted daughter with so much love for your parents. What ever you needed to share with your father before he traveled on–he knew! He needed to wait until his precious Sharon was with him. Such love! You are so special! You have been a loving daughter and have shared your heart and soul with your father and our Father.

I love you,
Peggy (Wolf)

Campbell's last note to his daughter Sharon:

Your Mother Said Here, get with
it & write a few Lines to your Girl.
We miss You very much & my Chickens
is Starving for Greens, So they have to starve
Im nibbling at the Raseberies Now & Then
Cutting out the old Canes, My Legs isnt
too strong Yet, But Im beleiving & trusting
for a full recovery, My back isnt giving me
No problems, but my Leg that the Vein was
taken out bothers me, But So what,
When we See the distruction, famins, flood
Storms & millions homeless I say God
forgive me to even consider to grumble.
Well sweatheart Mom & Dad Loves You &
miss you one & all, # Take Care
Love & Prayers.

Your first B'day away from home, we really miss you. Wish you were still here, have a good day, will be with you in our spirit.

Love you too much,
Dad & Mom
XXX

October 1998

An excerpt from THIS TIME
by Kenneth J. Holland

"A living, loving gospel sermon, however unlearned in matter and uncouth in style, is better than the finest discourse devoid of unction and power. A living dog keeps better watch than a dead lion, and is of more service to his master; and so the poorest spiritual preacher is infinitely to be preferred to the exquisite orator who has no wisdom but that of words, no energy but that of sound.

The like holds good of our prayers and other religious exercises; if we are quickened in them by the Holy Spirit, they are acceptable to God through Jesus Christ, though we may think them to be worthless things; while our grand performances in which our hearts were absent, like dead lions, are mere carrion in the sight of the living God."

Article was clipped by Gladys after Cam's death, original publication source unknown.

HIS LEGEND LIVES ON

You know how some of the great legends of our time live on? We never stop talking about Elvis Presley, Martin Luther King, or Abraham Lincoln. In the city of Yelm, the people never stop talking about Pastor Campbell Iverson.

Listening to his tapes and watching the videos of various events in his life always gave me chills. At times I felt as though he was speaking directly to me. The family told me that writing this book would be quite the experience for me. They were most definitely correct about that!

It wasn't until after Cam's death that the rest of the family learned he had flat out given away seven cars in his lifetime. He felt that if others needed them more than he did, they should have them. He never told anyone about it and he never accepted payment of any kind for those vehicles.

All of us get chills once in a while. While interviewing Cam's wife Gladys in her living room, I noticed that the lights would periodically flicker. Maybe it was just the wiring, as we were in an addition to the original house, but then again, maybe it wasn't.

I only make note of this happening because of a picture that his grandson Jon Bellows, Jr. shared with me when we first met. In the summer of 1998, he was using up a roll of film so that he could get it developed. He was just casually taking pictures around the living room in his home next door to his Grandparents' house.

Jon took the roll of film to a local pharmacy for developing. When he picked up the film the next day he noticed that there was more than just the living room in some of the pictures. There were unexplainable shadows and strange images included. These particular pictures and the negatives that they were made from were sent to the program "Unsolved Mysteries" in an effort to find out exactly what they were.

According to a specialist in the field, Jon had just had his first brush with the paranormal. These pictures are what are called in the paranormal world "broadcast imaging." The theory is that spirits can use the static charge from a television to produce their image. From what I have learned, the image can only be seen on the film after the shot is taken, meaning that you won't be able see them in the viewfinder.

The producers of the show wanted to do a segment about it, but Jon was hesitant. At the time, paranormal research was not as popular of a field as it is now. He didn't want to be viewed as a "freak." I have personally seen these pictures and they are quite amazing. You can clearly see Cam's face in the television that is turned off. The other images from a second photo show a reel-to-reel camera, a 1930's style lamp and a computer that is actually in the room behind the wall. The family is still trying to figure out what it all means!

There are many times when Gladys is out walking with the grandchildren and she is stopped on the streets. The people miss their shepherd; passersby often tell Gladys that they sure miss Pastor Cam. She always replies, "You are not the only one." Although I could feel the pain in that statement, she has a look of contentment in her eyes. She was happy to have the 44 years with her husband that she did. I can only hope that I am missed so dearly when I meet my maker.

LAURA M. PORRAS

Gladys strolling with her Grandchildren

Picture originally printed in the *Nisqually Valley News*
for Best Citizen 2003

Cam's Great, Great, Great, Great Grandfather said it best many years ago.

Tarald Olsen Gaupen, 4–10–1690–1773, was deeply religious and very godly. Being a poet and a composer of hymns, he was best known for a 150-page anthology of his works entitled: *En enfolding Legmands Tidsfordriv udi aandelige Sange og Rim* (a simple layman's contemplations of spiritual songs and rhymes).

His original piece follows, and then I have included a translation by Cam's nephew, Randal Carl Frivold.

Gud ske lov for nattens ende
Bliden dag vi har I hende
Give Gud vi kunde saa
Den anvende til din aere
I din fygt og sande laere
Og I troen harnisk staa.

*   *   *

May God be praised for the end of night
Close at hand is the day's first light
God, may it be that we
Use this day to your honor
In respect of you and your holy word
To stand firm in the faith.

AFTERWARD

The moral of the story is this: God never forgets. One woman's undying faith led an entire family to salvation and a small town to believe.

One of Cam's favorite sayings was as follows: Because Jesus is, I am. Because Jesus spoke, I speak. Because Jesus went, I go. Because Jesus gave, I give. Because Jesus did, I do.

I know what I am going to do with my life. Do you know what you will do with yours?

God Bless.

Cam would close almost every Sunday service and the many funeral services he officiated at challenging people to give their hearts to God. It went something like this:

Dear Jesus:

I am a sinner. Thank you for dying on the cross for my sins. Please forgive me, as I am truly sorry, and take all my sins away. I accept you as my own personal Savior, and now I am a child of God and have become "born again."

Thank you, Jesus.

REFERENCES

American War Bride Experience http://www.geocities. com/Heartland/Meadows/9710/WW2warbrides/facts.html

Cancer, Laetrile, Center for Holistic Life Extension, Dr. Luis Velazquez, Founder and Medical Director, http://www. extendlife.com/cancer9.html, accessed April 2004

Columbia Encyclopedia, Sixth Edition, Copyright © 2003 Columbia University Press

Fevered Lives - Tuberculosis in American Culture since 1870, by Katherine Ott, Harvard University Press, 1996 Cambridge, MA

Harold Manner Clinic, Tijuana, Mexico, The Cancer Cure Foundation, http://www.cancure.org/manner_clinic.htm, accessed April 2004

King's Cliffe - The 20th Fighter Group and the 446th. Air Group in the European Theater of Operations, Edited by: Maj. Edward J. Steiner (c) 1947, 1983, 1999 The 20th.Fighter Group Assoc., and "The 20th Fighter Wing, A History."

Laetrile Therapies/Manner Clinic–Laetrile - the answer to Cancer by James South MA, http://www.smart-drugs.net/ias-laetrile-cancer.htm, accessed April 2004

The Laetrile/B17 Cover-up, Pat Rattigan ND http://darrendixon.supanet.com/laetrile.htm accessed April 2004

Manner Metabolic Therapy, Stephen Barrett, M.D., July 1, 2001 http://www.quackwatch.org/01QuackeryRelatedTopics/Cancer/manner.html

Mother of Courage, video compiled by Nonna Childress Dalan, Produced at Sixth Christian Drama Workshop, Evangel College, 1111 N. Glenstone, Springfield, MO 65802, June 17, 1982, 8:30 PM–Adapted from letters to her children.

Speaking in Tongues -All About GOD Ministries, Inc.

7150 Campus Drive, Suite 320, Colorado Springs, Colorado 80920
719–884–2246, 719–884–2247 fax, Email: Questions-6.4@All-AboutGOD.com, Website: **AllAboutGOD.com** http://www.speaking-in-tongues.net/, accessed May 2004

Stanford Encyclopedia of Philosophy description of Miracles - Levine, Michael, "Miracles", The Stanford Encyclopedia of Philosophy (Winter 2002 Edition), Edward N. Zalta (ed.), h*ttp://plato.stanford.edu/archives/win2002/entries/miracles/,* accessed March 2004

Washington State Reformatory–Monroe Corrections Center http://www.doc.wa.gov/home.asp, http://www.doc.wa.gov/facilities/mccdescription.htm Site Updated 1/13/04

What Is The Laetrile Therapy - Site Ownership: Maria Hernandez Arz. nouel, #454, Santo Domingo, Dominican Republic
http://www.1cure4cancer.com/controlcancer/information/laetrile.htm, http://www.1cure4cancer.com/controlcancer/information/cytohist.html, accessed April 2004

A heartfelt "Thank You" goes out to Cam's daughter Sharon for all of her guidance and prayers during this process. She was my official "editor" for this book! Another thank you goes out to Jon Bellows, Jr., her son, for his encouragement along the way.

In everything give thanks. 1 Thessalonians 5:18

Contact author Laura M. Porras
or order more copies of this book at

TATE PUBLISHING, LLC

127 East Trade Center Terrace
Mustang, Oklahoma 73064

(888) 361 - 9473

Tate Publishing, LLC

www.tatepublishing.com

CONTACT INFORMATION:

lauramporras@yahoo.com
www.publishedauthors.net/lauramporras